Series / Number 07-031

MOBILITY
TABLES

MICHAEL HOUT
University of Arizona

SAGE PUBLICATIONS
Beverly Hills / London / New Delhi

*BOOK POCKET + CARDS
IN BACK OF BOOK.

For information address

SAGE Publications, Inc.
275 South Beverly Drive
Beverly Hills, California 90212

SAGE Publications India Pvt. Ltd.  SAGE Publications Ltd
C-236 Defence Colony   28 Banner Street
New Delhi 110 024, India   London EC1Y 8QE, England

International Standard Book Number 0-8039-2056-3

Library of Congress Catalog Card No. L.C. 83-060605

THIRD PRINTING, 1988

When citing a professional paper, please use the proper form. Remember to cite the
correct Sage University Paper series title and include the paper number. One of the
following formats can be adapted (depending on the style manual used):

(1) IVERSEN, GUDMUND R. and NORPOTH HELMUT (1976) "Analysis of Variance." Sage University Paper series on Quantitative Application in the Social Sciences,
07-001. Beverly Hills and London: Sage Pubns.

OR

(2) Iversen, Gudmund R. and Norpoth, Helmut. 1976. *Analysis of Variance*. Sage
University Paper series on Quantitative Applications in the Social Sciences, series no.
07-001. Beverly Hills and London: Sage Pubns.

CONTENTS

Series Editor's Introduction

Mobility Tables by Michael Hout reviews all of the most widely used methods for analyzing cross-classified data on occupational origins and destinations. It should not be thought, however, that the volume is of use only to sociologists, or to a subset of sociologists at that. As Professor Hout notes at the beginning and then expands on near the end, the models and methods of mobility analysis can be used in a wide variety of contexts. What distinguishes mobility tables is the identity between row and column categories. Since this feature is often found, the material reviewed and explained by Hout should find ready application in a number of settings and disciplines..

Chapter 1 introduces the basic ideas and tests designed to show whether or not there is perfect mobility (which there seldom is). Chapter 2 considers certain kinds of partial mobility, as when there is limited mobility in the very top or bottom categories. These models are special cases of a more general model, which is developed in Chapter 3. The material in this chapter assumes ordered categories, but it is important to note that not all analyses of mobility tables require this assumption. Chapter 4 covers a still more general model, one that incorporates rather complex conditions of mobility and stability. In Chapter 5, the focus changes slightly to that of socioeconomic achievement. The methods used in this analysis and the assumptions on which it is based differ from those of mobility research, as Hout makes clear at the outset. Chapter 6 then dicusses some very recent papers to show the reader the direction in which work on mobility tables is headed. Finally, Chapter 7 shows by example how the method of mobility tables can be applied to other areas.

Throughout the volume, care is taken to point out similarities and differences among models. To further that goal each model is applied to data on mobility from father's occupation to son's first occupation from Featherman and Hauser's 1973 study of the American labor force. Since it is expected that many readers will attempt to reproduce the results in the book as a means of understanding the models, results are presented in enough detail that interested researchers can validate their efforts. Although the book does not contain detailed instructions for implementing computer programs, computing advice is rendered in especially problematic cases.

Because of its thorough yet lucid coverage and because of the wide applicability of the methods beyond the confines of mobility research per se, *Mobility Tables* should be an important volume for a wide audience of students and researchers.

—*Richard G. Niemi*
Series Co-Editor

MOBILITY TABLES

MICHAEL HOUT
University of Arizona

1. ANALYZING MOBILITY TABLES

Social mobility is one of the most studied topics in social science. Interest in intergenerational mobility goes back to Marx and Weber, yet new findings and analytical developments come faster and more furiously in this field than in any other in sociology. This intense activity is warranted by mobility's place in our understanding of social stratification. Because the structure of intergenerational mobility gauges the persistence of material advantage from one generation to the next, answers to fundamental questions about opportunity, class, and privilege depend on the correct specification of that structure. To appreciate this point, compare the variety of conclusions about opportunity in capitalist society reached by Lipset and Bendix (1959: 57-60), Lenski (1966: 411-415), Blau and Duncan (1967: 432-441), Wright and Perrone (1977), Featherman and Hauser (1978: 481-495), Brieger (1981), and Hout (forthcoming).

Many methodological developments have advanced the study of mobility in the past fifteen years. Some of these advances are quite technical. While I have tried to keep technical detail to a minimum, at least a nodding familiarity with recent developments in the analysis of cross-classified data is necessary before some models can be appreciated. Fienberg (1980), Knoke and Burke (1980), and Clogg (forthcoming) are good introductory sources. On the other hand, the reader need not be up on the latest in latent structure models, quasi-uniform

AUTHOR'S NOTE: *I have benefited greatly from the comments of Clifford C. Clogg, Otis Dudley Duncan, Robert M. Hauser, and Michael E. Sobel on drafts of this book. Thanks to each of them for their help and advice. I am also grateful to Jo Migliara, who typed and retyped my manuscript, and to Sherry Cooksey, for her careful proofreading. The original research reported here was paid for by the University of Arizona.*

association models, or the like. When these models are relevant, they will be introduced as new material.

Developments in the study of mobility quickly pass to other fields—witness the diffusion of path analysis. The models presented in this monograph can be applied to any square table. Some nonmobility applications are covered in Chapter 7.

The Basics

Occupational mobility tables cross-classify persons according to their occupations at two points in time. The earlier point is usually referred to as the *origin*; the later point is known as the *destination*. Occupations are often ranked according to socioeconomic status, but ranking is a characteristic of some models of social mobility, not of the mobility table itself. The most common origin variable is the occupation of the subject's father while the person was growing up. A person's first occupation is another common origin variable. The most common destination variable is a person's current occupation. First occupation also may be used as a destination variable, as in most of the examples in this monograph. Mobility from father's occupation to subject's first or current occupation is *inter*generational mobility. Mobility from first to current occupation is *intra*generational mobility.

After selecting origin and destination variables, occupational categories must be defined and coded. This is a huge data reduction decision because occupational data can be coded in far more detail than current methods of mobility analysis can exploit (Hodge, 1981). Over 12,000 different occupational titles are coded in the Department of Labor's Dictionary of Occupational Titles (U.S. Department of Labor, 1977). That mass of detail must be reduced to a manageable number of occupational categories. Most large studies code occupations to the 441 occupational categories in the U.S. Census classification (Featherman et al., 1977). Even this number of categories is too large for the analysis of mobility tables.

Criteria for selecting an appropriate number of occupational categories are not well developed. The criteria used by most researchers mix theoretical and pragmatic concerns. If the purpose of the analysis is to investigate class boundaries as the pattern of mobility reveals them, categories should not combine persons of different classes. For example, the researcher must decide how to code foremen. The census category "craftsmen" includes both foremen and skilled workers. While foremen do more manual than white-collar work and share the socioeconomic status of the most skilled craftsmen (e.g., engravers, pressmen, locomotive firemen, aircraft mechanics, telephone repair-men, and tool and die makers), their tie to management puts them in a distinct class position.

Comparability with the coding procedures of past studies is another consideration. If detection of trends or replication of previous studies is an important goal, comparability is of paramount importance. In such instances the overriding concern should be to replicate the coding of others as closely as possible (e.g., Baron, 1980).

Five occupational categories will be used in most of the examples in this book. A few examples use seventeen categories. Figure 1 presents a diagram that shows the relationship between the five- and seventeen-category schemes. The categories commonly used in analyses of mo-bility in Great Britain are different, and the difficulty in reconciling them is a lesson in the importance of this first step (see Goldthrope and Hope, 1972).

Once the occupations are classified, analysis of the data can proceed. In most studies—and throughout this book—the same categories are used for origin and destination, and origin and destination categories are arrayed in the same order. The cells of the table give the counts of persons that share each combination of origin and destination. Let i

Upper Nonmanual	Professionals, self-employed
	Professionals, salaried
	Managers
	Salespersons, nonretail
Lower Nonmanual	Proprietors
	Clerical workers
	Salespersons, retail
Upper Manual	Craftsmen, manufacturing
	Craftsmen, other
	Craftsmen, construction
Lower Manual	Service workers
	Operatives, other
	Operatives, manufacturing
	Laborers, manufacturing
	Laborers, other
Farm	Farmers and farm managers
	Farm laborers

Figure 1 Five-Category and Seventeen-Category Classifications of Occupation

index the rows and j the columns; f_{ij} is the number of persons with origin i and destination j. When i and j are the same, origin and destination are the same (at least as far as the occupational classification in use can distinguish origins and destinations). These cells in which i = j form the main diagonal of the table. They are special cells because the subjects in them are immobile. The distinction between *mobile* and *immobile* subjects is very important for many of the models to be considered in later sections.

Occasionally mobility tables take a different form. Instead of reporting occupational origins and destinations, some researchers classify subjects as upwardly mobile, immobile, or downwardly mobile. This "mobility status" variable is then cross-classified by origins, destinations, or some other variable. *This is bad practice.* Mobility status often masks important relationships in the data by combining origins and destinations in a way that suppresses the correlation between them (Duncan, 1966; Boudon, 1975). For example, mobility is uncorrelated with education and father's occupation in most studies. Mobility status is an attempt to report data on mobility per se, circumventing the constituent origins and destinations. The problem is that the simplicity of mobility status often does violence to the pattern of the untransformed data.

Table 1 gives an example of a mobility table. This table cross-classifies father's occupation by son's first full-time civilian occupation for U.S. men 20 to 64 years of age in 1973. The diagonal cells are italicized. Most examples in this book refer to this table.

Sources of Mobility Data

Most mobility data come from surveys of members of the labor force. The U.S. Bureau of the Census collected data on mobility as supplements to the March Current Population Survey in 1962 (under the direction of Peter M. Blau and Otis Dudley Duncan) and in 1973 (under the direction of David L. Featherman and Robert M. Hauser). Data on intergenerational mobility are not part of the decennial census, but census data can be used in the analysis of intragenerational mobility as the 1970 Census collected data on prior occupations of a sample of individuals.

Another source of mobility data is the marriage record section of some states' vital records systems. Rogoff's (1953) analysis of marriage license records in Indianapolis is a pioneering study of intergenerational mobility.

TABLE 1
Father's Occupation by Son's First Occupation

Father's Occupation	Son's Occupation					
	Upper Nonmanual	Lower Nonmanual	Upper Manual	Lower Manual	Farm	Total
Upper Nonmanual	1,414	521	302	643	40	2,920
Lower Nonmanual	724	524	254	703	48	2,253
Upper Manual	798	648	856	1,676	108	4,086
Lower Manual	756	914	771	3,325	237	6,003
Farm	409	357	441	1,611	1,832	4,650
Total	4,101	2,964	2,624	7,958	2,265	19,912

SOURCE: Featherman and Hauser (1978: 49).

There have been too many mobility studies by independent investigators to catalogue here. Notable early efforts are Glass's (1954) study of mobility in Great Britain in 1949 and Lipset and Bendix's (1952) Oakland Mobility Study of that same year. A large-scale contemporary effort to collect data on mobility is the General Social Survey (NORC, 1980), which gathers data on intergenerational mobility on a regular basis.

Elementary Operations

The elementary procedures used to analyze any cross-classification are useful starting places in the analysis of mobility tables. Perhaps the most elementary operation for cross-classifications is the calculation of percentage distributions within rows or columns of the table. Table 2 presents the row percentages and column percentages for Table 1. It is customary to refer to the row percentages as *outflow* percentages and the column percentages as *inflow* percentages. The terms refer to the intergenerational flow of labor captured by the two sets of percentages. The outflow percentages record the distribution of destinations for each category of origin; the image is of labor flowing out of the given origin occupation. The inflow percentages record the distribution of origins for each destination; the image is of labor flowing into the given destination occupation. The U.S. data show substantial variation among occupations in both inflow and outflow. There are also large differences between inflow and outflow for particular occupational categories.

TABLE 2

Inflow and Outflow Percentages for Mobility from Father's
Occupation to Son's First Occupation

Father's Occupation	Son's Occupation					
	Upper Nonmanual	Lower Nonmanual	Upper Manual	Lower Manual	Farm	Total
Inflow Percentages						
Upper Nonmanual	34.5	17.6	11.5	8.1	1.8	14.7
Lower Nonmanual	17.7	17.7	9.7	8.8	2.1	11.3
Upper Manual	19.5	21.9	32.6	21.1	4.8	20.5
Lower Manual	18.4	30.8	29.4	41.8	10.5	30.1
Farm	10.0	12.0	16.8	20.2	80.9	23.4
Total	100.0	100.0	100.0	100.0	100.0	100.0
Outflow Percentages						
Upper Nonmanual	48.4	17.8	10.3	22.0	1.4	100.0
Lower Nonmanual	32.1	23.3	11.3	31.2	2.1	100.0
Upper Manual	19.5	15.9	20.9	41.0	2.6	100.0
Lower Manual	12.6	15.2	12.8	55.4	3.9	100.0
Farm	8.8	7.7	9.5	34.6	39.4	100.0
Total	20.6	14.9	13.2	40.0	11.4	100.0

Inflow and outflow percentages are informative at a very low level
of analysis. While they provide some information about the process of
social stratification, other processes related to the relative supply and
demand of labor power from different strata also influence the inflow
and outflow patterns. For example, the high fertility of farmers coupled
with a decrease in the proportion of the U.S. labor force in farming
contributes to the unbalanced inflow/outflow pattern for farm occupations. While only 39.4 percent of farmers' sons follow their fathers
into farming, 80.9 percent of farmers in 1973 have farm origins. One of
the objectives of the statistical modeling techniques to be covered in
this book is to control for extraneous forces like the redistribution of
the demand for labor in the U.S. (or other) economy, and differential
fertility.

Another elementary operation is the calculation of the index of dissimilarity between the outflow proportions for two origins or between
the inflow proportions for two destinations. The index of dissimilarity
is the sum of positive differences between two proportional distributions. For example, the index of dissimilarity between the outflow

TABLE 3

Indexes of Dissimilarity Between Pairs of Origins (below the
diagonal) and Destinations (above the diagonal) for Mobility
from Father's Occupation to Son's First Occupation

	Occupation				
Occupation	Upper Nonmanual	Lower Nonmanual	Upper Manual	Lower Manual	Farm
Upper Nonmanual	–	.169	.310	.353	.483
Lower Nonmanual	.163	–	.155	.192	.688
Upper Manual	.308	.200	–	.158	.640
Lower Manual	.384	.276	.157	–	.607
Farm	.499	.407	.367	.354	–

proportions for lower manual occupations and those for farm occupation is:

$$\Delta = .126 - .088 + .152 - .077 + .128 - .095 + .554 - .346 = .354$$

The index of dissimilarity measures the proportion of cases that would have to be reclassified in order to make the two sets of outflow proportions identical. Table 3 presents the index of dissimilarity for each pair of origins and destinations.

χ^2 Tests Applied to the Mobility Table

Another elementary operation in common use is the χ^2 test. The test of the null hypothesis of no association is routine in the analysis of cross-classified data, and it is certainly germane to the analysis of mobility tables. In fact, the model of statistical independence that underlies the χ^2 test has a substantive interpretation in the context of mobility table analysis.

Suppose that the distribution of origins is fixed by the labor demand conditions faced by the fathers and by differential fertility among origins. Suppose further that the distribution of destinations is fixed by the demand for different types of labor within the national economy. If sons or daughters are randomly assigned to destinations subject only to these two constraints on the marginal distributions, mobility is perfect in the sense that the odds on arriving at any one destination are

TABLE 4
Frequencies Expected Under Model of Perfect Mobility
from Father's Occupation to Son's First Occupation

| Father's Occupation | Son's Occupation | | | | | |
	Upper Nonmanual	Lower Nonmanual	Upper Manual	Lower Manual	Farm	Total
Upper Nonmanual	601.39	434.66	384.80	1,167.00	332.15	2,920
Lower Nonmanual	464.02	335.37	296.90	900.43	256.28	2,253
Upper Manual	841.54	608.22	538.45	1,633.00	464.78	4,086
Lower Manual	1,236.36	893.58	791.07	2,399.15	682.84	6,003
Farm	957.70	692.18	612.78	1,858.41	528.94	4,650
Total	4,101	2,964	2,624	7,958	2,265	19,912

completely determined by the marginal distribution of destinations: Destinations are independent of origins. This is why the familiar model of statistical independence is often called the *model of perfect mobility*. When mobility is perfect, each row of outflow percentages is the same, making the index of dissimilarity zero for each pair of origins (and for each pair of destinations). Of course, no empirical mobility table will have precisely the same proportional distribution in each row (or column). Therefore, the χ^2 test is invoked to determine whether or not the observed pattern of deviations from perfect mobility can be attributed to sampling error.

The first step in the χ^2 test for the model of perfect mobility is the calculation of frequencies expected under perfect mobility. This expected frequency is the same as would normally be calculated for a χ^2 test:

$$F_{ij} = n_i n_j / N \qquad [1]$$

where N is total sample size and n_i and n_j are origin and destination marginals, respectively. All that is special is the interpretation of the model of independence (no association) as a model of perfect mobility. Expected frequencies for the U.S. data are in Table 4.

The second step in the usual χ^2 test is to compare these expected frequencies with the observed frequencies according to the formula:

$$X^2 = \sum_i \sum_j (f_{ij} - F_{ij})^2 / F_{ij} \qquad [2]$$

In large samples this statistic is distributed approximately as χ^2 with $(R - 1)^2$ degrees of freedom if the null hypothesis is true (where R equals the number of rows [and columns] in the table). It is quite common to find references to equation 2 as "chi-square" itself. But although this statistic is distributed approximately as χ^2 when the null hypothesis is true and the sample is large, the formula for the χ^2 distribution is different. Thus I will designate the statistic in equation 2 as X^2. Another statistic that is distributed approximately as χ^2 under the same assumptions is commonly used as well:

$$L^2 = 2 \sum_i \sum_j f_{ij} \log (f_{ij}/F_{ij}) \qquad [3]$$

where log is the natural logarithm function. L^2 is quite different from X^2 in computation, but it too is distributed as χ^2 with $(R - 1)^2$ degrees of freedom if the null hypothesis is true and if the sample is large.

If the null hypothesis of perfect mobility is false, both X^2 and L^2 will be larger than the corresponding value on the χ^2 distribution. So the test of the model of perfect mobility consists of calculating X^2 and L^2 and comparing their values to the percentile value in a tabulation of the χ^2 distribution. If X^2 and L^2 are less than the number in the χ^2 table, we fail to reject the null hypothesis of perfect mobility; if X^2 and L^2 are both greater than the number in the table, we reject the null hypothesis of perfect mobility. If the number in the table lies between X^2 and L^2 (a rare outcome), the test is indeterminate.

L^2 is introduced not as a check on X^2 or to make an indeterminate outcome possible but because it can be decomposed into substantively and statistically interpretable components (X^2 cannot). In fact, L^2 is a superior statistic; X^2 is carried because it is so familiar. When these procedures are followed for the mobility data in Table 1, we find that $X^2 = 7166.77$ and $L^2 = 6170.13$ with 16 degrees of freedom. With 16 degrees of freedom, the 95th percentile of the χ^2 distribution is 26.30, so the null hypothesis of perfect mobility is rejected by a huge margin.

Another index of fit is the index of dissimilarity between observed and expected frequencies. While the index of dissimilarity does not test the null hypothesis of perfect mobility (or any other null hypothesis), its interpretation as the proportion of cases misclassified by the model is appealing. The index of dissimilarity between the observed frequencies in Table 1 and the expected frequencies in Table 4 is .201. Thus the model of perfect mobility misclassifies one-fifth of the cases in Table 1.

Odds Ratios

A not-so-elementary operation that will be important later on is the calculation of odds ratios for adjacent rows and columns. For a 2×2 contingency table, the association in the table can be measured by the odds ratio (or cross-products ratio):

$$\alpha = f_{11}f_{22}/f_{12}f_{21} \qquad [4]$$

or some transformation (e.g., the natural logarithm) of α (see Goodman, 1969a, 1969b, 1979a; Davis, 1974; Fienberg, 1980). α greater than 1.0 indicates a positive association; α less than 1.0 indicates a negative association. The association in a $R \times R$ table can be expressed in terms of the $(R - 1)^2$ odds ratios for the 2×2 subtables for pairs of adjacent rows and columns of the full table (Goodman, 1979a). The order of rows and columns is a substantive decision that affects the odds ratios. Goodman (1979a) refers to these 2×2 subtables as the "basic set" of subtables. All the other possible substables contain redundant information. Thus the $(R - 1)^2$ odds ratios of the form:

$$\alpha_{ij} = f_{ij}f_{i+1,j+1}/f_{i+1,j}f_{i,j+1} \qquad [5]$$

or their transformation capture all of association in the mobility table.

Notice that there are as many 2×2 subtables and αs as there are degrees of freedom in the test of the model of perfect mobility. This is no coincidence. Any model for the association in a mobility table can be characterized by the number of nontrivial αs it implies (an α is trivial if it is equal to 1.0). The model of perfect mobility implies that $\alpha_{ij} = 1.0$ for all i and j. In subsequent sections the pattern of αs implied by different models will be one basis for comparing models more complicated than the model of perfect mobility. The pattern of αs depends on the order of the categories. Not all orders are equally suitable for modeling. But when the "right" order is used, the αs can be useful. The observed odds ratios for the U.S. data are shown in Table 5. Notice that the four largest odds ratios are on the diagonal. That will be important when proposing more elaborate models.

Mobility Ratios

Before moving on to models that are more complex than the model of perfect mobility, I would like to dispose of the topic of mobility ratios. Invented by Goldhamer and popularized by Rogoff (1953) and

TABLE 5
Odds Ratios for Basic Set of 2 × 2 Subtables from Table 1

Origins Compared	Destinations Compared			
	5:4	4:3	3:2	2:1
5:4	1.964	.836	1.300	1.098
4:3	1.122	2.725	.707	.944
3:2	1.489	.639	2.203	1.106
2:1	.722	1.464	.847	15.954

Glass (1954), the mobility ratio for cell i, j is the ratio of the observed frequency for that cell to the frequency expected under the model of perfect mobility:

$$R_{ij} = f_{ij} / F_{ij} \qquad [6]$$

Although the R_{ij} are useful for exploratory analysis (e.g., Hauser, 1979), R_{ij} is more commonly used as a measure of the association between origins and destinations. Unfortunately, R_{ij} does not measure the strength of association.

The appeal of the mobility ratio as a purported measure of association is intuitive. As the ratio of an observed quantity to that expected when there is no association in the table, it suggests itself as an index of the extent of association. There are three reasons why it is not. First, as demonstrated by Blau and Duncan (1967: 93-97) and elaborated by Tyree (1973), tables with identical association between origins and destinations but different marginal distributions will necessarily have different mobility ratios. This is the most telling critique of the mobility ratio. The other two objections to mobility ratios relate to this feature.

The second objection is that mobility ratios are based on the model of perfect mobility—a model that fails to fit most empirical tables (Goodman, 1965, 1969b; Hauser, 1978, 1979, 1981). Because it is based on the wrong model, the mobility ratio reflects both systematic association and error. That is because cell frequencies are composed of marginal effects, systematic association, and errors (both measurement and sampling errors). The creators of the mobility ratio saw it as the ratio of systematic association to marginal effects. They did not recognize the existence or importance of errors.

Despite the presence of error in the numerator, mobility ratios may be acceptable measures of association between origins and destinations if errors are insignificant relative to systematic association and if the marginal effects estimated under the model of perfect mobility are unbiased estimates of the true marginal effects. These conditions seldom hold for real data.

The third objection is that, in practice, a researcher has no way of assessing the relative importance of error and systematic interaction without reference to a model that fits the data. Once a model that fits is found, the mobility ratio is not needed; the association is better described by the parameters of the model.

Hope (1981) defends the mobility ratio on the grounds that it always has the same value for a given table, while alternatives derive their value from the specific model fit. But it is the very insensitivity of the mobility ratio that is the problem. No matter what model is correct for a given mobility table, the mobility ratio is always the same. Therefore, it gives at best an imperfect clue as to the structure of association in the table (Hauser, 1979). Worse, it is often misleading. The mobility ratio should not be interpreted as a measure of association.

2. INDEPENDENCE IN PARTS OF THE TABLE

As discussed in the section on χ^2 tests in Chapter 1, the model of perfect mobility does not describe the U.S. mobility data in Table 1. I now move on to more complex models. The models to be considered specify perfect mobility for some combinations of origins and destinations but barriers to mobility for others. Within the zones of perfect mobility, destinations are statistically independent of origins, but significant association exists elsewhere in the table. Much of the recent literature on social mobility has addressed this very issue: the existence of perfect mobility between some occupational categories and the nature of the barriers between others (e.g., Hauser, 1978, 1979; Breiger, 1981).

The first place to look for barriers to mobility is along the diagonal of the mobility table. The differences between observed and expected frequencies for the U.S. data showed more immobility than is expected under the model of perfect mobility. This feature is common. Mobility studies have repeatedly shown "excess" immobility of this sort (e.g., Lipset and Bendix, 1959; Blau and Duncan, 1967; Featherman and Hauser, 1978). Goodman's (1961, 1965, 1968, 1969a, 1969b, 1972a) model of quasi-perfect mobility addresses the immobility issue, and it will be considered first. Generalizations of the model of quasi-perfect mobility that include off-diagonal constraints on upward or downward mobility will also be considered. These include a model that allows for barriers to mobility at the extremes of the status hierarchy (Goodman,

1965, 1972a; Pullum, 1975) and a model that allows for symmetrical barriers to mobility.

Quasi-Perfect Mobility Defined

To analyze tables with an excess of cases along the diagonal, several people (Blumen et al., 1955; Goodman, 1961, 1965, 1969a, 1969b; White, 1963) proposed models that distinguish mobility from immobility. Consider Goodman's version. According to this model, the observed pattern of mobility is the outcome of two separate processes. The first process—the immobility part—allocates a certain proportion of people ("stayers") to destinations that are the same as their origins. The second process—the mobility part—resembles perfect mobility because it allocates the remainder of the population to destinations without regard to their origins. Some of the people allocated according to this process may end up where they started; for them origin and destination are the same—just as they are for the stayers. The difference between these people and stayers is that while "stayers" do not leave their origin status because of forces not accounted for by the model, the others arrive by chance—just as the destinations of the movers are arrived at by chance.

Goodman's model is a refinement of the mover-stayer model devised by Blumen et al. (1955). The original *mover-stayer model* divided the population according to their destinations. All people whose destinations were the same as their origins were classified as stayers. According to this mover-stayer model, the only people allocated by chance are the people whose origins and destinations are different; perfect mobility is specified as conditional on the fact of movement. While Goodman's model of *quasi-perfect mobility* (QPM) shares many concerns with the mover-stayer model and its extensions (Singer and Spilerman, 1974, 1976), Goodman's treatment is more internally consistent—and more consistent with other mobility models. In the mover-stayer model, only stayers are immobile. Under QPM, some nonstayers are immobile by chance. They are allocated to a destination identical to their origin on the basis of perfect mobility. Otherwise there would be an impermissible association between origins and destinations for this group, which is supposed to be perfectly mobile (by definition, perfect mobility exists only when origins and destinations are independent).

A Log-Linear Model of Quasi-Perfect Mobility

Having specified the model verbally, I will now express it formally. To do so, the notation of log-linear models is introduced. The most general log-linear model for a two-way cross-classification such as a mobility table is:

$$\log(F_{ij}) = a_0 + a_{1i} + a_{2j} + b_{ij} \tag{7a}$$

where a_0 is the "grand mean," a_{1i} is the row effect, a_{2j} is the column effect, and b_{ij} is the interaction effect. These parameters are subject to the constraints:

$$\sum_i a_{1i} = \sum_j a_{2j} = 0 \tag{8a}$$

and

$$\sum_i b_{ij} = \sum_j b_{ij} = 0 \tag{8b}$$

In the absence of interaction effects (i.e., where $b_{ij} = 0$ for all i and j), we have the model of perfect mobility. If none of the $b_{ij} = 0$, the model is saturated; it uses all of the degrees of freedom in the table and fits all the observed data exactly. All of the models considered in the rest of this book fall between the model of perfect mobility and the saturated model. They put constraints on the b_{ij} without making them all zero. They seek to attain an acceptable fit without using up all of the degrees of freedom in the table.

The model in equation 7a may also be written in multiplicative form:

$$F_{ij} = A_0 A_{1i} A_{2j} B_{ij} \tag{7b}$$

subject to multiplicative constraints analogous to the additive constraints in equations 8a and 8b:

$$\prod_i A_{1i} = \prod_j A_{2j} = 1 \tag{8c}$$

and

$$\prod_i B_{ij} = \prod_j B_{ij} = 1 \tag{8d}$$

Parameters of the log-linear and multiplicative models are linked by the simple relationships: $a_{1i} = \log(A_{1i})$, $a_{2j} = \log(A_{2j})$, and $b_{ij} = \log(B_{ij})$, so when $B_{ij} = 1$ for all i and j, we have the model of perfect mobility, and under that condition equations 1 and 7b are equivalent. Only log-linear expressions for models are used throughout this book to save space.

The constraints in equation 8b are necessary only because there are more parameters than degrees of freedom in equation 7a. They make estimation of the saturated model possible because they render 2R − 1 of the estimated interaction parameters redundant. For the model of QPM, only the b_{ij} on the diagonal are not equal to zero. Fewer than $(R − 1)^2$ are nonzero, so the constraints in equation 10b are not needed. The log-linear equations for the model of QPM are:

$$\log(F_{ij}) = a_0 + a_{1i} + a_{2j} + b_i \qquad \text{for } i = j$$

$$\log(F_{ij}) = a_0 + a_{1i} + a_{2j} \qquad \text{for } i \neq j \qquad [9]$$

The constraints in equation 8a apply. The b_{ii} are the immobility effects. They are the only interaction parameters in the model. They measure the deviation of the diagonal cells from the pattern of perfect mobility. The equations for cells in which $i \neq j$ are identical to equations for the model of perfect mobility, except for the condition that i must not equal j. The model uses R more degrees of freedom than the model of perfect mobility—one for each b_{ii}—so the degrees of freedom are calculated by the formula:

$$df_{QPM} = (R − 1)^2 − R$$

Estimates of the F_{ij} under QPM are obtained by "blocking out" or deleting the diagonal cells and fitting the model of statistical independence to the remaining cells. However, because of the exclusion of the diagonal cells, equation 1 does not produce quasi-independent F_{ij} for the unblocked cells. In fact, except under special circumstances (see Bishop et al., 1975: 192-206), iterative methods are required.

Quasi-Perfect Mobility Results

QPM does not fit the U.S. data in Table 1 very well. L^2 and X^2 are in excess of what could be expected at any conventional significance level. The lack of fit of QPM does not mean that immobility is unimportant. L^2 and X^2 for QPM are much smaller than the corresponding statistics for the model of perfect mobility: The difference in L^2 is 5486.79. Recall that the model of perfect mobility misclassifies 20.1 percent of the cases in Table 1; QPM misclassifies 5.5 percent.

Estimates of the F_{ij} are in the top panel of Table 6. The diagonal entries are not F_{ij} but estimates of the number of persons who are immobile by chance ($F_{ii}*$). These estimates are obtained in the following way. In the preceding section the odds ratio was introduced. It was pointed out that under the model of perfect mobility, all odds ratios in the basic set of odds ratios for the mobility table are 1.0. Under QPM, perfect mobility holds for nonstayers. Thus the number of nonstayers in a diagonal cell is the number that will yield a value of 1.0 for every odds ratio in the basic set that involves that cell. Start in the middle of the table. The third diagonal cell is involved in four odds ratios in the basic set:

$$\alpha_{22} = F_{22}{}^*F_{33}{}^* / F_{23}F_{32} = 1.0$$

$$\alpha_{23} = F_{23}F_{34} / F_{24}F_{33}{}^* = 1.0$$

$$\alpha_{32} = F_{32}F_{43} / F_{33}{}^*F_{42} - 1.0$$

$$\alpha_{33} = F_{33}{}^*F_{44}{}^* / F_{34}F_{43} = 1.0 \qquad [10]$$

The first and last of these involve two unknown diagonal cells, but the middle two involve just one unknown: $F_{33}{}^*$. One or both of these can be used to estimate $F_{33}{}^*$; e.g., the second equation can be set equal to 1.0 and solved for $F_{33}{}^*$ to yield:

$$F_{33}{}^* = F_{23}F_{34} / F_{24}$$

$$= (321.81)\,(1645.78)/(914.55)$$

$$= 579.11$$

Then the first and last equations above can be solved for $F_{22}{}^*$ and $F_{44}{}^*$. They, in turn, yield estimates of $F_{11}{}^*$ and $F_{55}{}^*$ according to the following formulas:

$$F_{11}{}^* = F_{21}F_{12} / F_{22}{}^*$$

and

$$F_{55}{}^* = F_{45}F_{54} / F_{44}{}^*$$

Note that the calculations were carried out to more significant digits than are reported in this book, so your calculations may vary slightly from what is reported in Table 6 and in subsequent tables.

Estimates of the b_{ii} parameters (immobility effects in additive form) are in the second panel of Table 6. They were obtained using the formula:

$$b_{ii} = \log\,(f_{ii} / F_{ii}{}^*) \qquad [11]$$

Some programs, e.g., FREQ (Haberman, 1979), estimate the parameters directly, so these calculations may not be necessary. The

TABLE 6
Results for Quasi-Perfect Mobility Model of Mobility from Father's Occupation to Son's First Occupation

| | Destination | | | | |
Origin	Upper Nonmanual	Lower Nonmanual	Upper Manual	Lower Manual	Farm
(A) Expected Frequencies					
Upper Nonmanual	372.17	344.01	285.54	811.49	64.96
Lower Nonmanual	419.43	387.70	321.81	914.55	73.21
Upper Manual	754.79	697.68	579.10	1645.78	131.74
Lower Manual	934.37	863.67	716.88	2037.33	163.09
Farm	578.41	534.64	443.77	1261.18	100.96
(B) Parameter Estimates					
Upper Nonmanual	1.335				
Lower Nonmanual		.301			
Upper Manual			.391		
Lower Manual				.490	
Farm					2.898

$L^2 = 683.34$; $X^2 = 720.74$; df = 11; $p < .01$; $\Delta = .055$.
NOTE: Unless otherwise noted, parameter estimates in this and subsequent tables are in logarithmic form.

b_{ii} show that immobility to first jobs is greatest in the farm stratum ($b_{55} = 2.898$), followed by the upper nonmanual ($b_{ii} = 1.335$), lower manual, upper manual, and lower nonmanual strata, in that order. This order is not to be taken too seriously because the model does not fit these data. Note that b_{22} and b_{33} are very close and that b_{44} is not far from them.

Barriers to Mobility at the Top and Bottom: The Corners Model

QPM can be generalized to include blocking of cells not on the diagonal. Goodman (1965) and Pullum (1975) propose the hypothesis that the unacceptable fit of QPM is due to "excess" short-distance mobility at the extremes of the status hierarchy. The order of the categories must be known in order to define "short-distance" and "extremes of the status hierarchy." Mobility from upper to lower nonmanual and from lower to upper nonmanual is not so different from immobility within the upper and lower nonmanual strata as QPM predicts. The model also proposes that farmers' sons move into lower manual occupations with greater than expected frequency and that the reciprocal flow of lower nonmanual workers' sons into farming is greater than expected under QPM. This model does not have a commonly used name. I will refer to it as the *corners model*.

Formally, the corners model fits the R diagonal parameters fit by QPM plus four corner parameters for cells $(1,2)$, $(2,1)$ $(R - 1, R)$, and $(R, R - 1)$:

$$\log(F_{ij}) = a_0 + a_{1i} + a_{zj} + b_{ij}Z_{ij} \qquad [12]$$

where the a_{1i} and a_{zj} must sum to zero as in equation 8a, and $Z_{ij} = 1$ if $i = j$ or if (i,j) is a corner cell, i.e., cells $(1,2)$, $(2,1)$, $(R, R - 1)$, and $(R - 1, R)$. The additional parameters have the effect of equating observed and expected frequencies in the corner cells. Each $Z_{ij} = 1$ reduces degrees of freedom by one, so the corners model has $(R - 1)^2 - (R + 4)$ degrees of freedom.

Although in the context of the U.S. data the corners model fits the "excess" short-distance mobility, the model can fit shortfalls as well as excesses. The sign of the b_{ij} indicates whether cell (i,j) contains an excess or shortfall; a positive b_{ij} means there are more persons in cell (i,j) than would be expected under QPM, while a negative b_{ij} means that there are fewer persons than expected.

The corners model fits the U.S. data better than QPM does, but as Table 7 shows, it does not attain a fit that is acceptable at conventional levels of significance. The model fits the corner and diagonal cells exactly, so the entries for these cells are estimates of the number of men expected under perfect mobility $F_{ij}*$. The calculations are the same as above. For example, $F_{21}* = F_{31}F_{22}*/F_{32}$. Each parameter estimate is:

$$b_{ij} = \log (f_{ij}/F_{ij}*)$$

The parameter estimates must be interpreted with care because the model does not fit, but subsequent analysis will show that they are not far off. They show very high immobility in the farm stratum, decreased roughly half for immobility in the upper nonmanual stratum, and again by half for upward mobility from lower to upper nonmanual. There are five cells with intermediate parameter values of about the same value: the three remaining corner cells and the lower nonmanual and lower manual diagonal cells. Immobility in the upper manual stratum is barely more than can be expected on the basis of the marginal effects (subsequent analysis will show b_{33} to be insignificant).

TABLE 7
Results for Corners Model of Mobility from Father's
Occupation to Son's First Occupation

| | Destination | | | | |
| | Upper | Lower | Upper | Lower | |
Origin	Nonmanual	Nonmanual	Manual	Manual	Farm
(A) Expected Frequencies					
Upper Nonmanual	286.48	280.06	279.12	662.89	42.99
Lower Nonmanual	292.29	285.74	284.79	676.35	43.87
Upper Manual	727.22	710.92	708.56	1682.75	109.14
Lower Manual	826.90	808.37	805.69	1913.42	124.10
Farm	408.88	399.71	398.39	946.13	61.36
(B) Parameter Estimates					
Upper Nonmanual	1.597	.621			
Lower Nonmanual	.907	.606			
Upper Manual			.189		
Lower Manual				.553	.647
Farm				.532	3.396

$L^2 = 50.12$; $X^2 = 50.44$; df = 7; $p < .01$; $\Delta = .014$.

Symmetrical Association

QPM is an important baseline model in mobility analysis. Many researchers begin with QPM and add parameters as needed to attain an acceptable fit to the data. The corners model is the outcome of such a strategy. Another important baseline model starts by fitting an especially constrained interaction parameter to each cell. The special constraints require that all interactions be symmetrical (Goodman, 1968, 1972c; Knoke and Burke, 1980: 49-54):

$$F_{ij} = a_0 + a_{1i} + a_{2j} + b_{ij} \qquad [13]$$

where equations 8a and 8b apply and $b_{ij} = b_{ji}$. This model is known as the *model of quasi-symmetry* (QS). It allows the researcher to perform a global test of the symmetry of movement among occupational categories. If QS fits the data, no asymmetrical models need to be considered. If QS fails to fit, the researcher can add asymmetries one at a time in order to determine the minimal set of asymmetries.

Two models are closely related to QS. First, the *model of symmetry*

(S) constrains not only the interaction parameters; it also constrains the marginal effects to be symmetrical:

$$F_{ij} = a_0 + a_{1i} + a_{1j} + b_{ij} \qquad [14]$$

where equations 8a and 8b apply and $b_{ij} = b_{ji}$. Under S not only the marginal parameters but also the marginal totals are equal for origins and destinations.

The second related model is the *model of marginal homogeneity* (MH). Under MH the interaction effects are not symmetrical, but the origin and destination marginals are the same. This is not the same as equal marginal effects. Because the interaction effects are not symmetrical under MH, the marginal effects cannot be equal or the marginals themselves will not be. In fact, MH is not a log-linear model, but it can be tested using log-linear methods because its fit is the difference between the L^2 for S and the L^2 for QS.

Frequencies expected under S and QS and the fits of S, QS, and MH are shown in Table 8. None of the models fit. However, a com-

TABLE 8

Expected Frequencies for Models of Symmetry and Quasi-Symmetry of Mobility from Father's Occupation to Son's First Occupation

Origin	Destination				
	Upper Nonmanual	Lower Nonmanual	Upper Manual	Lower Manual	Farm
(A) Symmetry					
Upper Nonmanual	1414	622.50	550.00	699.50	224.50
Lower Nonmanual	622.50	524	451.00	808.50	202.50
Upper Manual	550.00	451.00	856	1223.50	274.50
Lower Manual	699.50	808.50	1223.50	3325	924.00
Farm	224.50	202.50	274.50	924.00	1832
(B) Quasi-Symmetry					
Upper Nonmanual	1414	575.88	289.06	599.01	42.06
Lower Nonmanual	669.12	524	264.16	752.30	43.42
Upper Manual	810.94	637.84	856	1657.81	123.40
Lower Manual	799.99	864.70	789.18	3325	224.13
Farm	406.94	361.58	425.60	1623.87	1832

	L^2	X^2	df	p	Δ
Symmetry	2804.87	2562.79	10	< .01	.118
Quasi-Symmetry	27.45	27.35	6	< .01	.011
Marginal Symmetry	2777.42	—	4	< .01	—

parison between QS and QPM reveals that nearly all of the off-diagonal association in Table 1 is symmetrical. Hauser (1981) shows that the introduction of a single asymmetry involving upward and downward mobility within the nonmanual strata—cells (1, 2) and (2, 1)—produces a model that fits quite well (L^2 = 7.79; X^2 = 7.78; df = 5; p = .26; $\triangle$ = .005). This last point demonstrates the utility of QS as a diagnostic model (see also Hauser, 1979). Duncan (1981) shows how to use S, QS, and HM in the analysis of panel data.

3. SOCIAL DISTANCE MODELS

The QPM and corners models considered in the preceding section are special cases of a general model developed by Goodman (1972a). In this section more members of this class are considered. These models order categories along a status or other dimension. In most cases the intervals defined by the ordering of occupational categories are assumed to be equal. But the principal assumption is that the odds on a given move are a function of the category boundaries crossed. Some of the models concern the number of category boundaries crossed. Others concern which categories are traversed. In either case, if the occupational categories are not clearly ordered, the model is not appropriate.

Constrained Diagonals Models

The models considered in this section derive from the *diagonals crossings model* (DC) proposed by Goodman (1972a: 661-671):

$$\log(F_{ij}) = a_0 + a_{1i} + a_{2j} + c_{ij} + d_k + u_{ij} \qquad [15]$$

where $\qquad k = i - j$

$$c_{ij} = \Sigma\, v_s \qquad \text{for } s = j \text{ to } i - 1 \text{ if } i > j$$

$$= i \text{ to } j - 1 \text{ if } i < j$$

$$u_{ij} = \log(f_{ij} - a_0 - a_{1i} - a_{2j} - d_k) \qquad \text{for } (i, j) \epsilon S$$

$$= 0 \text{ otherwise}$$

and equation 8a applies. The set S is composed of cells to be blocked out in a given model.

The simplest constrained diagonals model specifies a single parameter for all main diagonal cells (d_0), testing the proposition that immobility exceeds what would be expected on the basis of perfect mobility by the same proportion in all occupational categories:

$$\log(F_{ij}) = a_0 + a_{1i} + a_{2j} + d_0 \qquad [16]$$

where equation 8a applies. This model is labeled QPM-C for *quasi-perfect mobility (constrained)*. This model uses only one of the five possible d_k and none of the c_{ij} or u_{ij} parameters in equation 15, i.e., they are all set to zero. Two related models add parameters for the minor diagonals that are constrained in the same manner:

$$\log(F_{ij}) = a_0 + a_{1i} + a_{2j} + d_{|k|} \qquad [17]$$

where $|k| = |i - j| = 0$ or 1 and equation 8a applies. This model is symmetrical in the sense that the same parameter applies to the upper and lower minor diagonals. It is labeled SD-C for *symmetrical diagonals (constrained)*. The second model relaxes the symmetry:

$$\log(F_{ij}) = a_0 + a_{1,i} + a_{2,j} + d_0 + d_k \qquad [18]$$

where $k = i - j = -1, 0$, or 1 and equation 8a applies. This model is labeled D-C for *diagonals (constrained)*.

Four more models are defined by relaxing constraints on the main and then the minor diagonals, i.e., by adding u_{ij} terms. The first pair of models is obtained for equations 17 and 18 by relaxing the constraints on the main diagonal by adding the five possible u_{ii} terms. First:

$$\log(F_{ij}) = a_0 + a_{1i} + a_{2j} + d_{|k|} + u_{ij} \qquad [19]$$

Second:

$$\log(F_{ij}) = a_0 + a_{1i} + a_{2j} + d_k + u_{ij} \qquad [20]$$

where $(i, j) \in S$ if $i = j$ and equation 8a applies. These models are labeled QSD-C and QD-C, respectively; the Q stands for "quasi," indicating that the main diagonal is blocked out. The last two models relax the constraints on the minor diagonals:

$$\log(F_{ij}) = a_0 + a_{1i} + a_{2j} + d_{|k|} + u_{ij} \qquad [21]$$

where $\quad u_{ij} = u_{ji}$

and

$$\log(F_{ij}) = a_0 + a_{1i} + a_{2j} + d_k + u_{ij} \qquad [22]$$

where $(i, j) \,\epsilon\, S$ if $-1 \leqslant i - j \leqslant 1$ and equation 8a applies. These two models are known as QSD and QD. QSD is not a member of the general class of models defined by equation 15, but it is an acceptable generalization.

The similarities and differences among the seven models are displayed in Figure 2. The figure uses integers to designate interaction parameters or combinations of interaction parameters for each cell. If the integer in one cell equals the integer in another cell, the interaction parameter(s) for the two cells are the same. Goodman (1979b: 808) advocates the use of charts like this one "as a 'machine' for building models that take account of relevant substantive phenomena."

The results for all of these models are presented in Tables 9 and 10. The expected frequencies for selected models and goodness of fit for each model (and the models of perfect mobility [PM] and quasi-perfect mobility [QPM] for comparison) are in Table 9; the parameter estimates for all models are in Table 10. As shown in Table 9, none of the models fits the data at the .05 level. Note, however, that the size of the OCG-II sample contributes to the difficulties in finding a model that fits. The sample is simply so large that very small departures from expected frequencies prove to be significant. The importance of this qualifier is shown in the $\triangle$ column. While PM misclassifies 20.1 percent of the cases, QPM misclassifies only one-fourth as many cases (5.5 percent), QSD reduces that by a factor of four to 1.3 percent, and QD reduces it by half to less than 1 percent.

The first conclusion to be drawn from Tables 9 and 10 is that immobility is substantial, particularly at the extremes—upper nonmanual and farm. The negative u_{ij} are not indicative of "status disinheritance" (Goodman, 1965) because the u_{ij} are deviations from the corresponding d_k, and they are constrained to sum to zero, guaranteeing that some of them will be negative. The only instances of combined interaction effects $d_0 + u_{ii}$ less than zero are small negative sums in QSD and QD for the third diagonal cell.

The second conclusion is that the association between origins and destinations is quite symmetrical. The only comparison between a symmetrical model and a corresponding asymmetrical model that shows significant departure from symmetry is the last comparison ($L^2_{QSD} - L^2_{QD} = 18.09$; df = 4; p < .01). Examining the u_{ij} for those two models indicates that the biggest asymmetry is between cells (1, 2) and (2, 1). There appears to be more upward mobility from lower nonmanual to upper nonmanual strata than downward mobility across that same boundary. Another possible asymmetry indicated in the u_{ij} is between cells (4, 5) and (5, 4), but the small number of cases in

QPM-C

1				
	1			
		1		
			1	
				1

SD-C

1	2			
2	1	2		
	2	1	2	
		2	1	2
			2	1

D-C

1	2			
3	1	2		
	3	1	2	
		3	1	2
			3	1

QPM

1				
2				
	3			
		4		
				5

QSD-C

1	6			
6	2	6		
	6	3	6	
		6	4	6
			6	5

QD-C

1	6			
7	2	6		
	7	3	6	
		7	4	6
			7	5

QSD

1	6			
6	2	7		
	7	3	8	
		8	4	9
			9	5

QD

1	6			
7	2	8		
	9	3	10	
		11	4	12
			13	5

Figure 2   Displays of Interaction Parameters for Constrained Diagonals Models

(4, 5) means that the difference may not be significant. As noted in the section on Symmetrical Association in Chapter 2, the asymmetry between (1, 2) and (2, 1) is the only necessary asymmetry.

Status Barriers and Crossings Parameters

To this point the c_{ij} parameters in equation 15 have not been addressed. All of the diagonals models considered above leave the c_{ij} at

TABLE 9
Results of Constrained Diagonals Models for Mobility from
Father's Occupation to Son's First Occupation

	Destination				
Origin	Upper Nonmanual	Lower Nonmanual	Upper Manual	Lower Manual	Farm
(A) Expected Frequencies: QPM-C					
Upper Nonmanual	1305.68	334.77	193.18	831.09	255.28
Lower Nonmanual	372.39	814.64	160.94	692.37	212.67
Upper Manual	750.88	562.35	947.88	1396.07	428.82
Lower Manual	857.47	642.18	489.69	3523.97	489.69
Farm	814.58	610.06	352.04	1514.50	1358.03
(B) Expected Frequencies: SD-C					
Upper Nonmanual	1414.28	474.89	224.13	618.88	187.81
Lower Nonmanual	553.00	768.31	290.07	492.24	149.38
Upper Manual	615.02	683.51	1067.74	1449.41	270.32
Lower Manual	746.14	509.62	636.82	3576.80	533.62
Farm	772.56	527.67	405.23	1820.67	1123.87
(C) Expected Frequencies: QSD-C					
Upper Nonmanual	1414	481.92	243.66	718.48	61.95
Lower Nonmanual	590.48	524	361.34	715.49	61.69
Upper Manual	639.21	773.66	856	1717.68	99.45
Lower Manual	906.04	736.38	825.66	3325	209.92
Farm	551.27	448.04	337.34	1481.35	1832

	L^2	X^2	df	p	Δ
PM	6170.13	7166.77	16	<.01	.201
QPM-C	2480.14	2266.81	15	<.01	.125
SD-C	1955.97	1905.68	14	<.01	.112
D-C	1952.96	1902.62	13	<.01	.113
QPM	683.34	720.74	11	<.01	.055
QSD-C	333.80	333.00	10	<.01	.042
QD-C	327.85	327.79	9	<.01	.041
QSD	33.63	33.52	7	<.01	.013
QD*	15.54	15.48	3	<.01	.006

TABLE 10

Estimates of the Interaction Parameters of Constrained Diagonals
Models of Mobility from Father's Occupation to Son's First Occupation

Parameter	QPM-C	SD-C	D-C	QPM	QSD-C	QD-C	QSD	QD
d_o	1.072	1.197	1.194	1.083	1.262	1.256	1.226	1.233
d_{iu}	–	.487	.456	–	.398	.350	.233	.219
d_{id}	–	.487	.505	–	.398	.422	.233	.254
u_{11}	–	–	–	.252	.005	.005	.483	.444
u_{22}	–	–	–	–.782	–.776	–.767	–.734	–.736
u_{33}	–	–	–	–.692	–.479	–.491	–1.290	–1.311
u_{44}	–	–	–	–.593	–.552	–.550	–.694	–.690
u_{55}	–	–	–	1.815	1.800	1.802	2.237	2.293
u_{12}	–	–	–	–	–	–	.540	.378
u_{23}	–	–	–	–	–	–	–.506	–.521
u_{34}	–	–	–	–	–	–	–.388	–.348
u_{45}	–	–	–	–	–	–	.345	.492
u_{21}	–	–	–	–	–	–	.540	.648
u_{32}	–	–	–	–	–	–	.506	.535
u_{43}	–	–	–	–	–	–	–.388	–.449
u_{54}	–	–	–	–	–	–	.345	.335

zero. The constrained and unconstrained diagonals models are one kind of social distance model. They specify a mobility process that is governed by the *number* of occupational categories to be crossed. For example, in most diagonals models moves across one category boundary are regulated by the same parameter, either $d_{|k|}$ or d_k; therefore, the same parameter applies to moves from lower manual to upper manual and from lower nonmanual to upper nonmanual strata.

The simplest of these models does not fit the American data very well. The problem might be that the process is as complicated as the QD model says it is. On the other hand, the problem might be that the *number* of boundaries crossed is less important than *which* boundaries are crossed. Suppose that mobility is a process of clearing barriers to movement. Each barrier might be analogous to a step of fixed height. The diagonals models specify that regardless of where you start, the first step is $d_0 - d_1$ high, the second is $d_1 - d_2$ high, and so on. Suppose instead that each barrier's height is determined by which two categories it separates. Under this model the barrier between upper and lower nonmanual is one height (v_1), whether or not it is the first step, the barrier between lower nonmanual and upper manual is another height (v_2), and so on. By this reckoning the distance between two categories i and j is the sum of the intervening heights:

$$c_{ij} = \sum_{s=j}^{i-1} v_s \qquad \text{for } i > j$$

$$\sum_{s=i}^{j-1} v_s \qquad \text{for } i < j$$

as defined in equation 15. This is the *crossing parameters model* (CP):

$$\log(F_{ij}) = a_0 + a_{1i} + a_{2j} + c_{ij} \qquad [23]$$

where equation 8a applies. In the examples above, moves from upper nonmanual to lower nonmanual and from lower nonmanual to upper manual were considered. According to CP, the distance between upper nonmanual and upper manual occupations is the sum of the intervening distances, and the parameter governing moves from upper nonmanual to upper manual is: $c_{13} = v_1 + v_2$. CP is particularly interesting because of its potential for mapping interoccupational distances in a two-dimensional space. Because the parameter linking any two categories i and j is the sum of the parameters linking adjacent pairs of categories that lie between i and j, all categories can be said to lie on a single line. Johnson (1980: 123-130) develops this interpretation of the CP model into a compelling model of assortative marriage in the United States.

Another interesting property of CP is that immobility at the extremes of the status hierarchy is attributed to the status barriers that divide occupational categories, not to intrinsic immobility as in other models, i.e., CP fits cells (1, 1) and (R, R) exactly. Constrained and unconstrained parameters may be introduced to measure the significance of immobility in categories 2 through R − 1 that is not accounted for by the barriers that separate occupational categories. In the constrained form (QCP-C), a single immobility parameter d_0 applies to all cells on the main diagonal:

$$\log(F_{ij}) = a_0 + a_{1i} + a_{2j} + c_{ij} + d_0 \qquad [24]$$

where equations 8a and 15 apply. In the unconstrained form (QCP), diagonal cells 2 through R − 1 are each affected by a unique immobility parameter d_{0i}:

$$\log(F_{ij}) = a_0 + a_{1i} + a_{2j} + c_{ij} + d_{0i} \qquad [25]$$

where equation 8a applies and d_{0i} is defined for $2 \leqslant i \leqslant R - 1$ only. Haberman (1979: 519) gives a different but equivalent specification. He defines d_{0i} for all i and identifies the parameters by constraining $v_1 = v_2$ and $v_{R-1} = v_R$. Parameter estimation is more complex with CP and its variants than with any of the other models considered so far (consult Goodman, 1972a; Haberman, 1979).

The results are in Table 11. The first three panels are expected frequencies under CP, QCP-C, and QCP. The fourth panel presents the distances among occupational categories (c_{ij}) implied by the v_k from CP (above the diagonal) and QCP (below the diagonal). The models once again fail to fit the data at the .05 level. Nonetheless, the fit is quite good when the Δ are taken into account. CP misclassifies 2.1 percent of the cases; QCP lowers that percentage to 1.6. The uniform immobility constraint does not work; QCP-C does not improve over the fit of CP, and it is significantly worse than QCP.

The first thing of note is that CP and QCP do well with relatively few parameters. They account for the high immobility in upper non-manual and farm occupations by design. The only substantial difference between them concerns immobility in lower nonmanual and upper manual occupations. CP predicts too much immobility for the lower nonmanual occupations and too little for upper manual occupations (note that the negative sign for d_{02} does not indicate "status disinheritance" as it would in a diagonals model).

The widest gap separating two adjacent occupations is between lower manual and farm occupations. Next in order of magnitude is the gap between upper and lower nonmanual occupations. The other two barriers are modest; the barrier between lower nonmanual and upper manual occupations is slightly greater than that between upper and lower manual occupations.

Mobility Models in Logit Form

Log-linear models need not be written as formulas for expected frequencies. Equivalent expressions for expected logits (defined below) or odds-ratios exist for any log-linear model expressed as a formula for expected frequencies (Goodman, 1979b). Often the substantive implications of a model are more obvious when the model is transformed into a logit model. A logit is the log-odds on a high-status destination (j) relative to a lower-status destination (j + 1) given a fixed origin status (i):

$$\Phi_{ij}^{XY} = \log(F_{ij}/F_{i,j+1}) \qquad [26]$$

where X designates origin and Y designates destination.

An equation expressed in terms of logits states the effect of origins on destinations in the mobility table as specified by a given model more clearly than does the equivalent expression for expected frequencies. Although general equations are often too complicated to serve this

TABLE 11
Results for Three Crossings Parameters Models of Mobility from Father's Occupation to Son's First Occupation

Origin	Destination				
	Upper Nonmanual	Lower Nonmanual	Upper Manual	Lower Manual	Farm
(A) Expected Frequencies: CP					
Upper Nonmanual	1414	543.70	287.60	631.54	43.16
Lower Nonmanual	664.64	580.66	307.14	674.47	46.09
Upper Manual	781.96	704.35	776.95	1706.14	116.59
Lower Manual	847.10	763.02	841.67	3324.06	227.16
Farm	413.30	372.27	410.64	1621.79	1832
(B) Expected Frequencies: QCP					
Upper Nonmanual	1414	566.36	266.26	630.27	43.10
Lower Nonmanual	678.64	524	297.64	704.54	48.18
Upper Manual	744.00	694.09	856	1677.20	114.71
Lower Manual	849.49	792.80	809.00	3325	227.00
Farm	414.87	387.04	395.10	1620.99	1832
(C) Interstratum Distances: C_{ij} (CP above diagonal: QCP below diagonal)					
Upper Nonmanual	–	.426	.793	1.086	2.489
Lower Nonmanual	.423	–	.367	.660	2.063
Upper Manual	.811	.388	–	.293	1.696
Lower Manual	1.086	.663	.275	–	1.403
Farm	2.488	2.065	1.677	1.402	–

(D) Parameter Estimates

	Crossings				Diagonals		
	1	2	3	4	2	3	4
CP	.426	.367	.293	1.403	–	–	–
QCP-C	.417	.365	.283	1.392	.019	.019	.019
QCP	.423	.388	.275	1.402	–.189	.189	.018

	L^2	X^2	df	p	Δ
CP	89.91	90.95	12	< .01	.021
QCP-C	89.48	90.65	11	< .01	.021
QCP	64.24	64.67	9	< .01	.016

36

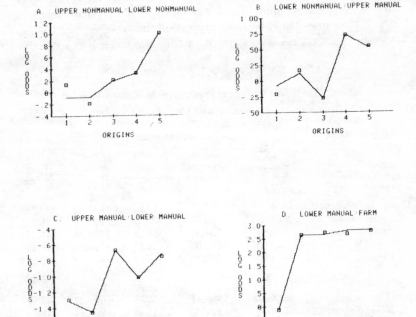

Figure 3: Observed Logits (symbols) and Logits Expected Under the QD Model (lines)

valuable heuristic purpose, equations for individual logits are informative. More important, graphs often add to our understanding of differences among models. The pattern of logits for U.S. men's first occupation is depicted in Figure 3. Observed logits are identified by the symbols; the logits expected under QD are connected by the lines. The graphs conform quite closely to the general patterns just described.

Simple models smooth the lines in various ways. The simplest model is the model of perfect mobility. Logits under this model have no slope against origins. QPM contains only diagonal effects, and it produces a sawtooth pattern in the logits. The corners model is dominated by peaks produced by the important diagonal effects, but has some additional slope due to the four off-diagonal effects. QCP not only has peaks for the diagonal effects but it also has a slope pattern that shows that logits for high-status destinations are more affected by origin status than are logits for lower-status destinations. Figure 4 contrasts the expected logits under QCP and QPM. Lines connect the logits for QCP; the symbols show the logits for QPM.

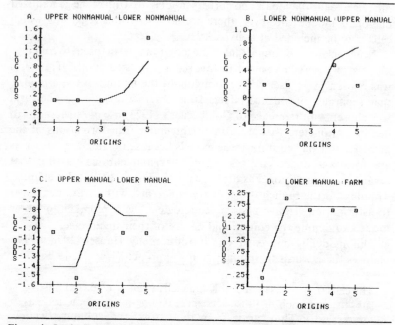

Figure 4: Logits Expected Under the QPM (symbols) and QCP (lines) Models

QCP fits the data best among these three models. Thus its image is the best description of the U.S. data encountered so far. It can be improved upon, and I turn now to models that fit as well as QCP and better.

4. TOPOLOGICAL MODELS

Hauser (1978, 1979; also Featherman and Hauser, 1978: 131-150) respecifies Goodman's (1972a) general model to allow for constraints that cross row, column, and diagonal boundaries. Hauser works with the u_{ij} parameters of equation 15 to develop topological models that define interactions in terms of quasi-independent subsets of cells ("levels") in the table. Each cell at a level is quasi-independent of the others at that level; i.e., there is no association between origins and destinations at a given level. No more than one interaction parameter applies to each cell (although the models may be reparameterized to include more than one parameter per cell; see Duncan and Schuman, 1980). All cells at the same level share a common interaction parameter, thus constituting a region of quasi-independence. In effect, this approach amounts to placing equality constraints on the parameters of models like the diagonals and corners models do. Unlike the generalized diagonals models, however, there are no restrictions regarding which cells may be included at a given level.

Nomenclature is important. The common term used to refer to models of the type covered in this section is "structural." This term was chosen by Hauser (1978) to highlight the feature of these models that separates prevalence effects from interaction effects. The term was chosen with reference to Goldberger's (1973) use of "structural" to denote parameters that were invariant under transformations of the data. Hauser picked it for these models because the interaction effects are invariant under changes in the marginal parameters. But that invariance is conditional as discussed in the last section of this chapter. Topology is the branch of geometry concerned with invariance under transformation. I have chosen "topological" as a moniker for these models to denote the conditional nature of their invariance.

This modeling approach was introduced by Hauser (1978, 1979). He uses these words to summarize his approach (Hauser, 1979: 416):

> The cells (i, j) are assigned to K mutually exclusive and exhaustive subsets, and each of those sets shares a common interaction parameter (d_k). Thus, aside from total, row, and column effects (i.e., marginal effects), each expected frequency is determined by only one interaction parameter, which reflects the density of mobility or immobility in that cell relative to that in the other cells in the table. The interaction parameters of the model correspond directly to the concept of joint density of observations [White, 1963: 26], and they may be interpreted as indexes of social distance between categories of row and column classifications [compare Rogoff, 1953: 31-32].

The subsets are composed of cells between which mobility is easy in the sense that origins and destinations are independent conditional on the marginal distributions and the assignment of cells to the K levels.

The Featherman-Hauser Model of Mobility to First Occupations

Featherman and Hauser (1978: 150-159; see also Hauser, 1979) propose a model with five levels (K = 5) for the data in Table 1. The level assigned to each cell is shown in the following design matrix:

$$\begin{matrix} 2 & 4 & 5 & 5 & 5 \\ 3 & 4 & 5 & 5 & 5 \\ 5 & 5 & 5 & 5 & 5 \end{matrix}$$

$$5 \quad 5 \quad 5 \quad 4 \quad 4$$
$$5 \quad 5 \quad 5 \quad 4 \quad 1$$

where the numbers designate the value of k. Note that the levels are numbered from highest to lowest density (relative to marginal effects). The numbers were assigned after the parameters were estimated. The model does not constrain the interaction parameters to any numerical order:

$$\log(F_{ij}) = a_o + a_{1i} + a_{2j} + d_k \qquad [27]$$

where equation 8a applies.

Only differences between levels parameters (d_k) are identified. That is, knowing $K - 1$ parameter values makes it possible to derive the Kth, so some restriction is necessary before levels parameters can be estimated. One consequence of this identification problem is that there are $(R - 1)^2 - (K - 1)$ degrees of freedom under the model (not $[R - 1]^2 - K$, as might be supposed). The normalization in equation 8b solves the identification problem, but it is not the only permissible restriction. For this model the zero-sum normalization is replaced by the restriction that one of the $d_k = 0$ (i.e., one of the levels is deleted from the calculations), and all others are measured as deviations from this baseline level. In practice the deleted level is the one that applies to the subset with the most cells. This restriction facilitates comparisons among models that include different numbers of cells in a given subset. Under the restriction in equation 8b, the value of d_k changes whenever the number of cells in subset k changes from one model to another, even if none of the differences $d_k - d'_k$ change from one model to the other. This undesirable property of the zero-sum normalization is not shared by the method of deleting one of the d_k. This principle will be illustrated in the last section of this chapter.

The K subsets do not exhaust the regions of quasi-independence in the table. Under special conditions, 2×2 subtables composed of cells from different levels can also exhibit no association between origins and destinations in the expected frequencies. For example, the 2×2 subtable composed of cells (1, 2), (1, 3), (2, 2), and (2, 3) contains cells from levels 4 and 5, yet the log-odds ratio of the expected frequencies for that subtable is zero:

$$\theta_{12} = \log(F_{12}F_{23}/F_{13}F_{23})$$
$$= d_4 + d_5 - d_4 - d_5 \qquad [28]$$

Results for this model are in Table 12. The expected frequencies are just that; none of them are analogous to the $F_{ij}*$ in preceding tables. Parameter estimates were obtained directly from FREQ (Haberman, 1979), but they can be derived from the expected frequencies by finding frequencies expected for each cell as if that cell were at level 5 ($F5_{ij}*$) and computing the ratio:

$$d_k = \log(F_{ij}/F5_{ij}*) \qquad [29]$$

The $F5_{ij}*$ are found in the same way the $F_{ij}*$ were found. By definition, odds ratios that involve expected frequencies for cells that are all at the same level are always equal to one. To obtain $F5_{ij}*$ for a cell not at level 5, form an odds ratio that involves cell (i,j) and three cells at level 5, e.g.,

$$F5_{22}* = F_{32}F_{23}/F_{33}$$

or some cells at level 5 and some $F5_{ij}*$ that have already been obtained.

The parameter estimates, however obtained, show that the pattern of mobility and immobility discerned in the parameter estimates from the diagonals model is also reflected in this set of parameter estimates. The

TABLE 12
Results for Five-Level Model of Mobility from Father's
Occupation to Son's First Occupation

	Destination				
Origin	Upper Nonmanual	Lower Nonmanual	Upper Manual	Lower Manual	Farm
(A) Expected Frequencies					
Upper Nonmanual	1414	515.08	297.43	649.06	44.41
Lower Nonmanual	724	522.95	301.97	658.97	45.09
Upper Manual	754.23	740.04	777.93	1697.62	116.16
Lower Manual	812.27	796.98	837.79	3328.23	227.73
Farm	396.35	388.89	408.80	1624.01	1832
(B) Parameter Estimates					
Upper Nonmanual	1.590	.599	0	0	0
Lower Nonmanual	.905	.599	0	0	0
Upper Manual	0	0	0	0	0
Lower Manual	0	0	0	.599	.599
Farm	0	0	0	.599	3.402

$L^2 = 66.57$; $X^2 = 66.50$; df = 12; $p < .01$; $\Delta = .018$.

largest parameter is for immobility in the farm stratum, followed by immobility in the upper nonmanual stratum, followed by mobility from lower to upper nonmanual. This last level (3) is the only asymmetrical level assignment in the model. Featherman and Hauser (1978: 152) note that "this asymmetry is striking because it suggests the power of upper white-collar families to block at least one type of status loss." The asymmetry may also be interpreted as evidence of the relative ease of intergenerational advancement within the broad nonmanual stratum. Featherman and Hauser's interpretation would be more tenable if density in cell (1, 2)—representing downward mobility for upper non-manual sons—was atypically low. It is not. The atypical density is in cell (2, 1), which suggests that it is the upward mobility of lower non-manual sons that is uncommonly high.

The interactions in the broad band of near-equality for mobility and immobility near the corners found in both the diagonals and corners models are here constrained to equality. The remaining 17 cells are marked by relatively low density (net of marginal effects), and move-ment among this large group of cells (which includes the entire third row and column—including the diagonal cell) is quasi-perfect, as is movement among the five cells at level 4 and between levels 4 and 5 at most points.

Featherman and Hauser's model does not quite fit. In fact, the corners model, the diagonals model, and several constrained diagonals models all have lower L^2 and X^2. Featherman and Hauser prefer this five-level model because the candidates for the sixth level do not improve the fit very much, nor do they form substantively compelling subsets of cells. Nonetheless, a number of respecifications of the Featherman-Hauser model are explored here for illustrative purposes. In following the analysis the reader is cautioned that the sample is very large (N = 19,912), so these methods are capable of detecting effects so small that they are likely to be difficult to interpret, given the current state of mobility theory.

Issues in Revising Models: Fit and Parsimony

As with other log-linear models, both descriptiveness (goodness of fit) and parsimony (degrees of freedom) are important in choosing a preferred model from among several mobility models. While a saturated model that uses all the degrees of freedom in a table will always describe the observed frequencies perfectly, such a description is little improve-ment over simple examination of the observed frequencies. Because of the tradeoff between parsimony and descriptiveness, "a simple model is often preferred over a more complicated one that provides a better fit" (Fienberg, 1980: 56). The difficulty is deciding how much loss of fit is too much in order to gain a few degrees of freedom.

The choice of a preferred model is guided by the additive property of L^2: *The difference between two L^2 with df_1 and df_2 degrees of freedom is distributed as χ^2 with $df_1 - df_2$ degrees of freedom.* This principle is applied in the analysis of log-linear models when one model implies another, i.e., when one model in some ways constrains one or more of the parameters of another. Constraints can take many forms but the most common are zero constraints and equality constraints. Zero constraints are imposed by setting one or more parameters of a log-linear model to zero. Equality constraints are imposed by setting the values of one or more parameters of a log-linear model equal to the value of another parameter in that model. This principle cannot be applied to the selection of a preferred model without reservations. Problems of overfitting, simultaneous inference, and indeterminate results make it impossible to select a preferred model on purely statistical grounds (see Fienberg, 1980: 56-68). Nonetheless, these methods provide useful guidelines, and they are introduced as an aid to model selection—not as hard and fast rules for picking a preferred model.

The Featherman-Hauser model implies the corners model and QD because the Featherman-Hauser model can be obtained from the other two by a series of zero and equality constraints. Furthermore, the corners model implies QD. Recall that QD was obtained by blocking out four cells left free by the corners model: (2, 3), (3, 2), (3, 4) and (4, 3). That is the same as saying that the corners model is a special case of QD in which u_{23}, u_{32}, u_{34}, and u_{43} are all constrained to be zero. The Featherman-Hauser model can then be obtained from the corners model by employing both a zero constraint and several equality constraints:

$$d_{33} = 0$$

$$d_{12} = d_{22} = d_{44} = d_{45} = d_{54} = d_4$$

Note that the distinction between zero constraints and equality constraints is somewhat indeterminate because it depends on the normalizations employed to identify the parameters. In log form Featherman and Hauser's specification may be written $d_5 = 0$, $\Sigma d_k = 0$, so that my zero constraint is then an equality constraint:

$$d_{13} = d_{14} = d_{15} = \ldots = d_{53} = d_5$$

There is a contraint for every degree of freedom separating two hierarchical models. Thus the difference two hierarchical models can be partitioned into ($df_1 - df_2$) separate tests, each with a single degree of freedom. Models can be modified by incorporating constraints that do not diminish fit at some conventional level of significance (say .05) and leaving out those that significantly reduce the fit. It is extremely important to note at this point that stated levels of significance are not accurate assessments of the probability of finding a L^2 of given magnitude under the null hypothesis because in most instances the null hypothesis was chosen to maximize the obtained L^2. This is classic overfitting and should be avoided in practice. In a real research setting some subset of the tests performed here could be performed to arrive at an acceptable model, but it would be bad practice to perform an equal number of tests and then take the stated probability levels as reflections of the true probabilities.

The model selection process is illustrated in Table 13. QD is at the top of the table. A series of four constraints is imposed in turn to lead from QD to the corners model. First, u_{43} is set to zero. Then u_{34} is set to zero, followed by u_{32} and u_{23}. Three of the four constraints significantly increase L^2. The only statistically trivial constraint that the corners model imposes on the diagonal is the one imposed on u_{34}.

The order in which the constraints are imposed is not unique. There are 4! = 24 orders. More important, there is no guarantee that two different orders will produce the same results. The situation is analogous to the indeterminacy of stepwise regression. The order in which the constraints are introduced can influence the outcome (Goodman, 1972c). That point is illustrated below when the decision about treatment of cell (3, 3) depends on which model is the baseline against which constraints on cell (3, 3) are evaluated.

Five constraints are necessary to convert the corners model into the Featherman-Hauser model. Table 13 begins with the only zero constraint: $d_{33} = 0$. Imposing this constraint on the corners model increases L^2 by 15.04 (see line C5), so d_{33} appears to be significantly different from zero. The remaining four constraints pool the five cells that compose level 4 of the Featherman-Hauser model. None of these constraints significantly increases L^2 (lines C6-C9). Thus the transition from the diagonals model to the Featherman-Hauser model involves some trivial and some consequential constraints. Consequential are the constraints that cells (4,3), (3,2), (3,3), and (3,4) are part of level 5. Together they account for 49.45 of the 51.03 difference in L^2 between the diagonals model and Featherman and Hauser's five-level model.

This information can be used to improve the fit of the Featherman-Hauser model. Note, however, that at this point the danger of over-

TABLE 13

Hierarchy of Models Linking the Diagonals Model and Five-Level
Model of Mobility from Father's Occupation to Son's First Occupation

Model		L^2	X^2	df	p	Δ
M1	Diagonals Model	15.54	15.48	3	< .01	.006
M2	$d_{43} = 0$	23.08	22.79	4	< .01	.007
M3	$d_{34} = 0$	23.25	22.98	5	< .01	.007
M4	$d_{32} = 0$	43.80	44.12	6	< .01	.012
M5	$d_{23} = 0$ (Corners Model)	50.12	50.44	7	< .01	.014
M6	$d_{33} = 0$	65.16	65.31	8	< .01	.017
M7	$d_{12} = d_{22} = d_4$	65.20	65.38	9	< .01	.017
M8	$d_{44} = d_4$	65.39	65.45	10	< .01	.017
M9	$d_{45} = d_4$	66.22	66.27	11	< .01	.017
M10	$d_{54} = d_4$ (Five-Level Model)	66.57	66.50	12	< .01	.018
M11	$d_{33} = d_6$	52.10	52.21	11	< .01	.015
M12	$d_{32} = d_{23} = d_7$	33.21	33.14	10	< .01	.012
M13	$d_{34} = d_{43} = d_8$	21.16	20.90	9	.01	.009
M14	$d_{23} = d_{32} = d_{34} = d_{43} = d_7$	29.90	29.69	10	< .01	.013
M15	$d_{23} = d_{32} = d_6; d_{34} = d_{43} = d_7; d_{33} = 0$	21.56	21.30	10	.02	.009
M16	$d_{23} = d_{32}; d_{34} = d_{43}$	20.78	20.50	8	.01	.009

Comparison

		L^2	X^2	df	p	
C1	M1-M2	7.54	7.31	1	< .01	
C2	M2-M3	.17	.19	1	> .50	
C3	M3-M4	20.55	21.14	1	< .01	
C4	M5-M4	6.32	6.32	1	< .01	
C5	M6-M5	15.04	14.87	1	< .01	
C6	M7-M6	.04	.07	1	> .50	
C7	M8-M7	.19	.07	1	> .50	
C8	M9-M8	.83	.82	1	> .50	
C9	M10-M9	.35	.23	1	> .50	
C10	M10-M11	14.47	14.29	1	< .01	
C11	M11-M12	18.89	19.07	1	< .01	
C12	M12-M13	12.05	12.24	1	< .01	
C13	M14-M13	8.74	8.79	1	< .01	
C14	M15-M13	.40	.40	1	> .50	
C15	M15-M16	.78	.80	2	> .50	

fitting is acute. Hauser (1979: 452-426) considers these cells to be sources of potential improvements but does not pursue them because of the overfitting issue. The first constraint relaxed is the one that puts cell (3,3) in level 5. A model that fits the third diagonal cell exactly as level 6 (M11) is a significant improvement over the Featherman-Hauser model (line C10). The next change relaxes the constraint that places cells (2,3) and (3,2) in level 5 and adds a new level (7) that contains just these cells. As line C11 shows, this change significantly reduces L^2. Finally, cells (3,4) and (4,3) are freed from level 5. Recall that the constraint $u_{34} = 0$ did not change L^2 significantly, but following Featherman and Hauser's preference for symmetry, cells (3, 4) and (4, 3) are both introduced, and the constraint that they be at the same level is tested in turn (see line C15). Adding an eighth level that contains cells (3, 4) and (4, 3) is a significant improvement over M12 (see line C12). Levels 7 and 8 cannot be pooled into a single level (M14) as shown in line C13. However, now that the surrounding minor diagonal cells are out of level 5, cell (3, 3) can be returned to that level (M15), as shown in line C14. Note that M15 is hierarchical to M13 not M14. The last test involves the symmetry of levels 7 and 8. Separate tests were made, but only a summary test is presented because the results are trivial. The combined L^2 from the two constraints is .78 (line C15).

Results from M15 are in Table 14. Compare the parameter estimates with those for QD (Table 10). The pattern of mobility revealed is pretty much the same. The advantage of M15 over QD is parsimony. M15 purges QD of trivial differences among parameters (there are six equality constraints in M15) and deletes one trivial parameter (d_{33}). M15 reveals less mobility across the manual/nonmanual boundary than the Featherman-Hauser model predicts ($d_7 = -.248$). This point is also evident in QD, but the diagonals model does not make it clear that the dearth of upward and downward mobility is of equal magnitude. Less intense is the shortfall of upward and downward mobility between skilled and other manual occupations. Of course, the stated significance level for M15 is lower (.02) than a level that is normally deemed acceptable. Further improvements in fit could be obtained by adding new levels. But going on in this fashion is not advisable. The chances of capitalizing on random errors in the data are very large at this point.

I would be inclined to agree with Featherman and Hauser that five levels are sufficient if I did not find the low density of mobility across the manual/nonmanual boundary very interesting, particularly in light of the findings of Featherman and Hauser (1978: 166-172) that show similarly low density for downward (but not upward) mobility across this boundary in their analysis of mobility from father's occu-

46

pation to son's current occupation. The seven-level model indicates that mobility opportunities for men of middle-status origins are less than Featherman and Hauser's (1978: 178) interpretation of their five-level model suggests.

The logit form for the five-level model and its seven-level extension are presented graphically in Figure 5. The symbols indicate the logits expected under the five-level model; the lines connect logits expected under the seven-level model. These figures show very clearly the ways in which the seven-level model is an improvement over the five-level model. Notice the similarity between the logits for the five-level model and those for the quasi-crossings parameters model in Figure 4. This observation is due to Pontinen (1981). The causes and consequences of the similarity are the topic of the next section.

Indeterminacy of Topological Models

There is more than one way to write most log-linear models. Goodman (1972a) provides formulas for generating equivalent expressions for most of the models considered to this point. Equivalent forms of a given model usually have equivalent substantive interpretations—but not always. Consider the two modifications of the Featherman-Hauser

TABLE 14
Seven-Level Model of Mobility from Father's Occupation
to Son's First Occupation (M15)

Origin	Upper Nonmanual	Lower Nonmanual	Upper Manual	Lower Manual	Farm
			Destination		
(A) Expected Frequencies					
Upper Nonmanual	1414	508.60	301.38	652.96	43.06
Lower Nonmanual	724	540.12	249.73	693.42	45.73
Upper Manual	781.79	652.27	865.35	1662.95	123.64
Lower Manual	798.60	853.92	784.05	3345.78	220.65
Farm	382.59	409.09	423.48	1602.86	1832
(B) Parameter Estimates					
Upper Nonmanual	1.647	.558	0	0	0
Lower Nonmanual	.918	.558	−.248	0	0
Upper Manual	0	−.248	0	−.120	0
Lower Manual	0	0	−.120	.558	.558
Farm	0	0	0	.558	3.410

$L^2 = 21.56$; $X^2 = 21.30$; df = 10; $p < .02$; $\Delta = .009$.

47

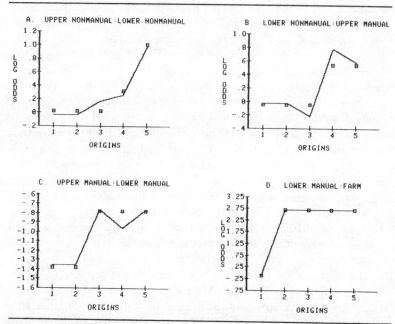

Figure 5: Logits Expected Under the Five-Level (symbols) and Seven-Level (lines) Topological Models

five-level model (which will be referred to as FH5 in this section) proposed by Pontinen (1981):

2	4	4	5	5			2	4	5	5	5
3	4	4	5	5			3	4	5	5	5
5	5	4	5	5			4	4	4	4	4
5	5	4	4	4			5	5	5	4	4
5	5	4	4	1			5	5	5	4	1

P1   P2

P1 was obtained from FH5 by shifting all the cells in the third column from level 5 to level 4, and P2 was obtained by a similar shift of all cells in the third row. FH5, P1, and P2 appear to be distinct models. They are not. All three models have the same expected frequencies.

The differences among FH5, P1, and P2 suggest different substantive interpretations. An important feature of FH5 is the expanse and symmetry of level 5. Featherman and Hauser (1978: 151-153) stress both elements in their interpretation of FH5. The greater symmetry of FH5 is not coincidental. Featherman and Hauser purposefully select the most symmetrical model (Featherman and Hauser, 1978: 150-176; Hauser, 1978, 1979, 1981). The symmetry is particularly important for their rejection of Blau and Duncan's (1967: 58-67) conclusion that semi-permeable class boundaries permit upward mobility from manual to nonmanual occupations and from farm to manual occupations but block downward mobility across those boundaries. P1 and P2 contain some of the symmetries of FH5 but not the crucial one between upward and downward movement between upper manual and lower nonmanual occupations. In P1 downward mobility from lower nonmanual to upper manual exceeds the reverse upward flow; in P2 upward mobility across the manual-nonmanual exceeds downward mobility across that boundary in a pattern consonant with Blau and Duncan's conclusion. Thus the fit of FH5 to the data in Table 1 cannot be used to test Blau and Duncan's conclusion about semipermeable class boundaries because equivalent models contradict the symmetry of FH5.

The relationships among FH5, P1, and P2 are revealed in the parameter estimates in Table 15. Most striking is the fact that the interaction parameters are identical for the three models. The marginal effects are very similar as well. The row marginal parameters are identical for FH5 and P1; the column marginal parameters are identical for FH5 and P2. The differences are confined to the parameters for the third row (P2) or column (P1). The third row parameter for P2 is .599 less than the corresponding parameter for FH5 and P1. The difference is the same for the third column parameter for P1. It is no coincidence that the interaction effect for level 4 is .599. Although Pontinen (1981: 6) arrives at P1 (and P2) by a rather complex set of operations, they are equivalent to adding the level 4 parameter to the third column (or row) and subtracting it from the marginal effect for that column (or row). The expected log-frequencies (and logits and odds ratios) do not change because the same quantity that is added to the interaction effect is subtracted from the column (or row) marginal effect.

P1 and P2 are not the only modifications of FH5 that yield the same expectations. Macdonald (1981) proposes the following level specification:

$$
\begin{array}{ccccc}
2 & 2 & 2 & 3 & 3 \\
4 & 2 & 2 & 3 & 3 \\
5 & 3 & 2 & 3 & 3
\end{array}
$$

$$5 \quad 3 \quad 2 \quad 2 \quad 2$$
$$< \quad 5 \quad 3 \quad 2 \quad 2 \quad 1$$

M1

M1 is obtained from P1 by subtracting .99 (i.e., $d_1 - d_4$) from the level parameters for the first column and adding that amount to a_{21}. The parameter estimates for M1 are also in Table 15. Notice that these parameter estimates are relative to level 3. That is to facilitate comparisons with FH5, P1, and P2. The comparison of parameter estimates in this form (rather than in the form presented by Macdonald, 1981: 559) points up the operations that produce M1 from P1 or, in two steps, yield M1 from FH5.

These results are troubling, but not so troubling that topological models should be abandoned as Macdonald (1981) claims. They do point up the caution that is necessary for appropriate interpretation of parameters of these models. Note that in three of the four equivalent models, differences in level parameters for cells within the same column are unaffected by the transformations that distinguish them. Similarly, for two of the four models, the differences are invariant within rows.

TABLE 15
Comparison of Parameter Estimates from Various Five-Level Models
of Mobility from Father's Occupation to Son's First Occupation

Effect		H5	P1	P2	M1	CP*
Row	1	−.318	−.318	−.318	−.318	.315
	2	−.303	−.303	−.303	−.303	.119
	3	.643	.643	.044	.643	−.432
	4	.718	.718	.718	.718	−.904
	5	−	−	−	−	−
Column	1	1.872	1.872	1.872	2.862	.965
	2	1.853	1.853	1.853	1.853	.451
	3	1.903	1.304	1.903	1.304	.201
	4	2.683	2.683	2.683	2.683	1.281
	5	−	−	−	−	−
Interaction	1	3.403	3.403	3.403	3.403	.495
	2	1.590	1.590	1.590	.599	.300
	3	.905	.905	.905	−	.300
	4	.599	.599	.599	−.086	1.402
	5	−	−	−	−.989	.306

Models can and do differ substantively despite the fact that the imply the same set of observed frequencies. That does not mean that log-linear methods are inappropriate for analyzing mobility data, nor does it mean that the researcher should ignore other evidence that one model is preferable to another. Hauser (1981) notes that similarity between this situation and the decision problems faced by researchers analyzing covariance matrices with structural equations models. For example, a researcher may be interested in the relationship between achievement motivation and academic performance among high school students. Once it has been established that the association between motivation and performance is not zero, four models of that association can be proposed. Motivation may cause performance, performance may cause motivation, they may cause one another, or the association may be a spurious results of correlated measurement errors. All four models imply the same covariance matrix, yet we deny neither the importance of exploring the equivalent models nor the need for deciding among the alternatives. So it is with equivalent log-linear models.

The models cannot be distinguished on fit. They all produce the same expected frequencies, so fit is the same for all of them. But fit is not the only criterion for preferring one model over another. Hauser (1981) argues for symmetry as a desirable quality of mobility models and demonstrates that FH5 contains the one asymmetry that is necessary and sufficient to account for the departure of the American data from quasi-symmetry (see the section on Symmetrical Association in Chapter 2).

Models may also be distinguished in replication. Equivalent models will not behave the same when subjected to tests involving comparisons over time, across national boundaries, or among subpopulations of one society. For example, suppose that P1 is the "true" model of mobility from father's occupation to son's first occupation. If the barrier between levels 4 and 5 in P1 were reduced to zero (i.e., the interaction effect for all cells in level 4 were reduced by .599), only P1 would detect the change as a simple change in one interaction parameter. All other models would produce specious changes in marginal parameters and—in the case of M1—some changes in interaction parameters as well. Parsimony dictates the selection of the model that exhibits the fewest parameter changes. Thus in this hypothetical case we would select P1 as the preferred model. Of course, replications with real data may not produce such clear-cut results. Nonetheless, temporal, cross-national, and subgroup comparisons can provide important clues as to the preferred model. An example of using cross-national comparisons for deciding between models is presented in the section on Equivalent Models in Chapter 5.

Before moving on to other topics, one last point on equivalence must be made. Equivalences between topological and other types of models are possible. Pontinen (1981) develops a very interesting one. He proposes a modified crossings parameter model that is equivalent to FH5. His model places equality constraints on the second and third crossings parameters ($v_2 = v_3$) and introduces a special parameter for cell (2, 1). The parameter estimates for this model (labeled CP*) are in the last column of Table 15. The first four v_i are listed as the first four interaction parameters; the parameter for cell (2, 1) is listed as the fifth. These results are quite different from the results for the other equivalent models. First of all, topological and crossings models emphasize different substantive processes. The topological models are more discrete. They focus on clusters of unordered and unconstrained interactions. The crossings models focus on status barriers that depend on the order of categories and on the constraints in equation 25. Both models highlight the excess of short-distance over long-distance mobility. But even in this respect they differ. Topological models could just as easily fit data that exhibit an excess of long-distance mobility; crossings models can only fit data with an excess of short-distance mobility.

5. SCALED MODELS OF ASSOCIATION

The analysis of mobility tables addresses the same theoretical issues as does the study of intergenerational effects on socioeconomic achievement (e.g., Blau and Duncan, 1967; Featherman and Hauser, 1978). Yet the two research traditions typically differ markedly in their approaches to data, as Hauser (1978) and others (e.g., Pullum, 1975: 2; Duncan, 1979) have observed. In contrast to the emphasis on patterns of high and low association in mobility subtables found in mobility analysis as described so far, the socioeconomic achievement approach emphasizes the magnitude of the causal impact of origins on destinations. These differences are reflected in the methodologies typical of the two schools. Log-linear models for tabular data are appropriate for the cell-by-cell scrutiny of mobility table analysis, while the general linear model better suits the multivariate approach of achievement research.

The issue of scaling occupational properties also divides attainment and mobility research. Mobility table research most often involves few assumptions about scale (although some models do presume order among the categories). For achievement research the choice of an appropriate scale is essential because the focus is on the relationship between a father's position on a scale of occupational prestige, status, or authority and his son's position on that scale. Yet Duncan (1979) has reconciled the two approaches by applying Simon's (1974) model to the mobility table and developing a constrained version of it. These models are extended by Goodman (1979a).

Uniform Association

The socioeconomic achievement approach to mobility posits a linear relationship between origins and destinations. The model states that an increase of one unit in the status of origin results in a specified increase in the status of destination (plus or minus a normally distributed error term). Suppose that this model is correct. Suppose further that the status scale has been divided into R equal intervals and the appropriate R × R cross-classification of origins by destinations had been constructed with the highest category first (i = 1; j = 1) and the lowest last (i = R; j = R) in both the row and column arrays. Under such conditions, the odds on one destination (j) relative to the next lower destination (j + 1) given origin i is (Haberman, 1979: 396-397):

$$\Phi_{ij} = \log (F_{ij} / F_{i,j+1})$$
$$= a_{2j} - a_{2,j+1} + bi \qquad \text{[30a]}$$

where equation 8a applies and b is the uniform association parameter (and under certain conditions, equal to the regression coefficient). The similarity between uniform association and regression can be seen in Figure 6, which plots the observed and expected logits obtained by fitting uniform association to the U.S. data (observed logits are plotted as symbols; expected logits as lines).

Note that uniform association produces logits that increase linearly with each increase in origin. The lines are parallel with a slope of b = .269. There are other similarities between uniform association and regression that are beyond the scope of this treatment (see Haberman, 1979: 396ff.; Logan, 1983). The model does not fit the U.S. data very well. Ways of improving fit will be discussed after alternative ways of writing the model are presented, but from Figure 6 it is apparent that immobility is the biggest problem.

The formula for expected frequencies under uniform association is:

$$\log(F_{ij}) = a_0 + a_{1j} + a_{2j} + bij \qquad \text{[30b]}$$

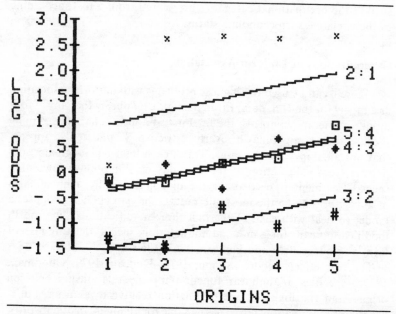

Figure 6: Observed Logits (symbols) and Logits Expected Under Uniform Association (lines)

where equation 8a applies. The model derives its name from the pattern log-odds ratios it implies:

$$\theta_{ij} = \log(F_{ij}F_{i+1,j+1} / F_{i+1,j}F_{i,j+1})$$

$$= b \qquad [30c]$$

That is, the association between origins and destinations is the same in every 2×2 subtable in the basic set of subtables. The uniform association model is a special case of Haberman's (1974) linear-by-linear interaction model:

$$\log(F_{ij}) = a_0 + a_{1i} + a_{2j} + bX_iX_j \qquad [31]$$

where equation 10a applies and X_i and X_j are scores for the row and column variables. The uniform association model is obtained from the linear-by-linear interaction model by setting X_i and X_j equal to any set of equally spaced constants. The specification used here is:

$$X_i = (R + 1) - i \qquad \text{and} \qquad X_j = (R + 1) - j \qquad [32]$$

so that the occupational categories are scored from 5 to 1, according to their relative socioeconomic status.

Generalizations of Uniform Association

Figure 6 can be used to diagnose problems with uniform association as a model for the U.S. data. From the figure it appears that any of four modifications may improve the fit. First, it appears that constraining the lines to be straight may be overly restrictive. Second, it also appears that not all slopes are the same. Third, each logit has its greatest departure from expectation at the log-odds on immobility, suggesting special treatment is needed for the diagonal. Finally, men of farm origins appear to be the most aberrant. Goodman (1979a) proposes a model to deal with each of the first three modifications. The fourth modification calls for a more ad hoc solution, such as deleting men of farm origin (see Blau and Duncan, 1967: 135ff.).

The row effects model (Simon, 1974; Duncan, 1979; Goodman, 1979a) specifies a nonlinear function for the relationship between origins and the logit for one destination relative to another, but it constrains that relationship to be the same for all logits. In other words, the row effects model says that the log-odds on a higher-status destination relative to the next lower-status destination change by a fixed amount for each shift of origins, regardless of the pair of destinations being compared. In logit form the row effects model is:

$$\Phi_{ij} = \log(F_{ij}/F_{i,j+1})$$
$$= a_0 + a_{2j} - a_{2,j+1} + b_0 X_i + b_{1i} \qquad [33]$$

where equations 8a and 32 apply and $b_{11} = b_{1R} = 0$. The restrictions on b_{11} and b_{1R} satisfy the identification problem (Goodman, 1979a). Other identifying restrictions are possible (Clogg, 1982b), but I prefer these because the resultant estimates of b_{12} through $b_{1,R-1}$ have a meaningful geometrical interpretation. Draw a line from Φ_{1j} to Φ_{Rj}; label it line AB_j. The slope of line AB_j will be equal to b_0. The coefficients b_{12} through $b_{1,R-1}$ measure the deviations of Φ_{2j} through $\Phi_{R-1,j}$ from line AB_j. Note that although the model allows the expected logits to deviate from the straight lines AB_j, the model does constrain the AB_j to be parallel and the deviations from AB_j, i.e., b_{1i}, are the same for all j. Thus the curves for two logits are equidistant at all points. This can be seen in panel A of Figure 7.

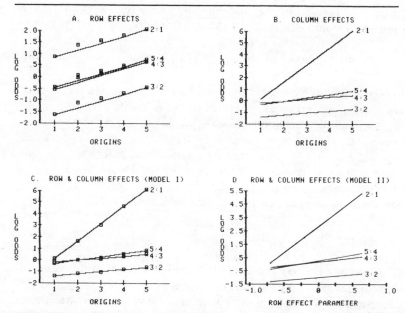

NOTE: Symbols in panels A and C represent deviations from straight lines due to row effects.

Figure 7: Logits Expected Under Models of Association

The column effects model (Goodman, 1979a) relaxes the constraint on slopes while maintaining linearity as seen in its application to the U.S. data in panel B Figure 7. This model contains parameters that shift the slopes of the lines connecting expected logits:

$$\Phi_{ij} = a_{2j} - a_{2,j+1} + (b_0 + b_{2j} - b_{2,j+1})\, X_i \qquad [34]$$

where equations 8a and 32 apply and $b_{21} = b_{2R} = 0$. As in the case of the row effects model, the extreme coefficients are set to zero to identify the others. In this case the restriction is imposed for symmetry and not because the coefficients have straightforward interpretations.

The row and column effects can be combined by adding them together. The result is a model (named Model I by Goodman) that allows departures from linearity that are measured by the b_{1i} (for $i = 2$ to $R - 1$) and shifts in the slopes of the lines AB_j connecting l_j to R_j

that are measured by the differences $b_{2j} - b_{2,j+1}$ for $j = 2$ to $R - 1$. The row and column effects model (Model I) is:

$$\Phi_{ij} = a_{2j} - a_{2,j+1} + (b_0 + b_{2j} - b_{2,j+1})\, X_i + b_{1i} \qquad [35]$$

where equations 8a and 32 apply and $b_{11} - b_{1R} = b_{21} = b_{2R} = 0$. Panel C of Figure 7 plots the logits expected for the U.S. data under this model.

An interesting possibility arises when the row and column effects are equal, i.e., when $b_{1k} = b_{2k}$ (for $i = k$, $j = k$, and $2 \leqslant k \leqslant R - 1$). This model is less important in the case of intergenerational mobility than in the modeling of other kinds of tables, e.g., the cross-classification of husbands' and wives' occupations (Hout, 1982). This model is known as the homogeneous row and column effects model (Model I).

Model II

Goodman (1979a) and Clogg (1982b, 1983) discuss a different perspective on modifying the constraints of the uniform association model. Rather than focusing on the possibility of entering nonlinearities or shifts in slope, they consider rescaling origins, destinations, or both in order to produce linear-by-linear interactions that have straight, parallel lines. Goodman (1979a) labels the model in equation 35 Model I, and proposes as an alternative (Model II):

$$\Phi_{ij} = a_{2j} - a_{2,j+1} + bu_i(v_j - v_{j+1}) \qquad [36]$$

where equation 10a applies, and

$$\Sigma u_i = \Sigma v_j = 0$$
$$\Sigma u_i^2 = \Sigma u_j^2 = 1 \qquad [37]$$

In this model, u_i is a set of scale adjustments for the origins, and v_j is a corresponding set for the destinations. Both are to be estimated from the data. This is a version of the linear-by-linear interaction model in which the scores for occupational categories are to be estimated instead of supplied by theory or prior research. If scores for occupational categories are unknown, Model II will estimate the scores that produce the best-fitting linear-by-linear interaction. If the u_i and v_j turn out to be evenly spaced (i.e., $u_i - u_{i+1}$ equals some constant for all i, and $v_j - v_{j+1}$ equals the same constant for all j), Model II will be the same as uniform association. If just the u_i are equally spaced, Model II is the same as the column effects model (equation 34); likewise, if just the v_j are equally spaced, Model II is the same as the row effects model (equation 33). Row and column effects (Model II) for the U.S. data are shown graphically in Panel D of Figure 7. The most obvious feature of this figure is the rescaling of the X-axis, which reflects the u_i. The lines are not parallel. The rescaling introduced by the v_j could be applied to the ij to make the lines parallel. Note that Model II is not log-linear because b, u_i, and v_j must all be estimated. Estimation is beyond the scope of this book (consult Goodman, 1979a; Clogg, 1983).

Analogous to the homogeneous version of Model I that constrains the row and column effects to be equal is a homogeneous version of Model II. This model is especially important substantively because it posits that the origin and destination scales are the same, i.e., that $u_k = v_k$ (for $i = k$, $j = k$, and $2 \leqslant k \leqslant R - 1$).

To this point nothing has been said about degrees of freedom. Actually, these models are quite parsimonious; they summarize the association between origins and destinations without spending many degrees of freedom. The parsimony is especially evident in large tables (e.g., Breiger, 1981; Hout, forthcoming). Uniform association is the most parsimonious; it fits the marginal distribution and *one* additional parameter. The row effects model and the column effects model each fit $R - 2$ additional parameters, as do the two homogeneous row and column effects models. The Model I and Model II row and column effects models fit the most parameters—$2(R - 2)$—which is nonetheless quite parsimonious. Subtracting the number of independent parameters from the degrees of freedom left after fitting the marginals $(R - 1)^2$, yields the following:

Model	Degrees of Freedom
Uniform Association	$(R - 1)^2 - 1$
Row Effects	$(R - 1)(R - 2)$
Column Effects	$(R - 1)(R - 2)$
Row & Column Effects (I)	$(R - 2)^2$
Homogeneous R&C (I)	$(R - 1)(R - 2)$
Row & Column Effects (II)	$(R - 2)^2$
Homogeneous R&C (II)	$(R - 1)(R - 2)$

TABLE 16
Results for Association Models of Mobility from Father's Occupation to Son's First Occupation

Origin	Destination				
	Upper Nonmanual	Lower Nonmanual	Upper Manual	Lower Manual	Farm
(A) Expected Frequencies: UA					
Upper Nonmanual	1407.07	647.02	320.36	483.31	62.24
Lower Nonmanual	778.96	468.87	303.89	600.12	101.16
Upper Manual	894.95	705.14	598.23	1546.45	341.23
Lower Manual	734.60	757.64	841.38	2847.06	822.33
Farm	285.42	385.33	560.14	2481.07	938.05
(B) Expected Frequencies: Model I					
Upper Nonmanual	1348.01	579.03	345.33	646.21	1.42
Lower Nonmanual	746.52	437.43	319.05	742.53	7.47
Upper Manual	842.18	686.74	624.92	1845.22	86.94
Lower Manual	864.02	864.14	864.69	2855.13	555.02
Farm	300.26	396.67	470.01	1868.91	1614.14
(C) Expected Frequencies: Model II					
Upper Nonmanual	1311.81	564.52	331.18	708.98	3.47
Lower Nonmanual	700.94	426.31	313.36	795.50	16.88
Upper Manual	862.63	695.04	613.66	1789.46	125.21
Lower Manual	987.70	923.79	898.88	2821.03	371.60
Farm	237.91	354.34	466.93	1843.04	1747.79

	L^2	X^2	df	p	Δ
Null	6170.13	7166.77	16	< .05	.205
Uniform Association	2280.69	2220.56	15	< .05	.120
Row Effects	2080.17	2042.67	12	< .05	.123
Column Effects	903.84	1680.36	12	< .05	.069
RC Model I	877.81	1824.29	9	< .05	.067
RC Model II	685.51	990.02	9	< .05	.065
Homogeneous Model I	1287.89	1343.50	12	< .05	.089
Homogeneous Model II	935.87	1056.91	12	< .05	.083

Analysis of Association in the U.S. Data

Table 16 summarizes the analysis of association in the U.S. data. The perfect mobility model (null association) is presented for comparison. None of these models fits well enough. That is not to say that the models are uninformative. They account for much of the association

TABLE 17
Parameter Estimates for Association Models of Mobility
from Father's Occupation to Son's First Occupation
(Standard Errors in Parentheses)

Parameter	UA	Row Effects	Column Effects	Row and Column Effects			Homogeneous Effects	
				I	IIa	IIb	I	IIb
Uniform	.269* (.005)	.295* (.006)	.525* (.011)	.534* (.011)	4.574	.269	.389* (.007)	.269
Row								
1	–	0	–	0	.642	5	0	5
2	–	.064* (.020)	–	-.030 (.021)	.271	3.469	.032* (.005)	3.950
3	–	.113* (.016)	–	-.079* (.018)	-.031	2.225	.155* (.009)	3.178
4	–	.221* (.016)	–	-.003 (.017)	-.191	1.565	.321* (.011)	2.736
5	–	0	–	0	-.691	-.493	0	.065
Column								
1	–	–	0	0	.456	5	0	5
2	–	–	.236* (.019)	.253* (.021)	.252	4.161	.032* (.005)	3.950
3	–	–	.593* (.026)	.615* (.029)	.119	3.613	.155* (.009)	3.178
4	–	–	.940* (.031)	.960* (.035)	.019	3.200	.321* (.011)	2.736
5	–	–	0	0	-.845	-.362	0	.065

NOTE: Standard errors could not be calculated for Model II.
*p < .05.

in the table with few parameters. The biggest improvement in fit is gained with the introduction of the single, uniform association parameter; the L^2 for uniform association is 2,280.69 less than L^2 for null association. Both row and column effects significantly improve fit. The row effect parameters are not equal to the column effect parameters as the difference between the L^2s for homogeneous and nonhomogeneous row-column models shows.

The parameter estimates for these models are in Table 17. The models do not fit well enough to assign substantive significance to the parameter estimates, but hypothetical interpretations can be advanced for didactic purposes. The UA parameter in the uniform association and row effects models is the slope of the line connecting Φ_{ij} and Φ_{Rj}:

In the column effects model and Model I the UA parameter is the baseline slope that is shifted by the column effects; in Model II it is the slope of the line connecting Φ_{ij} and Φ_{Rj} after the scale adjustments. A number of identifying restrictions can be placed on Model II. Table 17 shows two normalizations. Model IIa uses the one described above (equation 37). Model IIb constrains the UA parameter to be equal to the UA parameter in the uniform association model, and the row and column effects for upper nonmanual are constrained to equal 5.0. The second normalization highlights the interpretation of Model II as a scale adjustment on uniform association. The row and column effects can be interpreted as empirically derived scores for the rows and columns. If these row and column coefficients were known in advance they could replace (5, 4, 3, 2, 1) as the row and column scores. Fitting the linear-by-linear interaction model with these scores for the rows and columns would yield the same L^2 as Model II did and a UA parameter of b = .269. It is desirable to apply the same scores to the row and column categories since they refer to the same occupations, but identical scores cannot be used for rows and columns without significant reduction of fit because the homogeneous Model II does not fit as well as the unconstrained Model II.

The lack of homogeneity may be due to the interaction of exogenous factors that lead to the poor fit of Model II. But if the model did fit and if row and column scores still were not homogeneous, we could conclude that distances among occupations had changed over the generation or that the composition of the occupational categories is different for fathers and sons. For the U.S. data I would be inclined to accept the second interpretation over the first because significant changes in the U.S. labor force have produced a number of differences among the occupational distributions of fathers and sons within the broad categories of the 5×5 table; e.g., 35 percent of the fathers in the upper nonmanual category are salaried professionals while 67 percent of sons and 80 percent of fathers in the farm category are farmers and farm managers compared to 25 percent of sons.

Analysis of Association with the Diagonal Deleted

The task of improving the fit of these models begins where we began before: on the diagonal. As with other log-linear models, the association models considered in this section can be modified by blocking out certain cells or (equivalently) by fitting unique parameters to those cells. Taking the latter approach, the quasi-uniform association model is given by:

$$\Phi_{ij} = a_{2j} - a_{2,\,j+1} + b_0 X_i + d_i(Z_{ij} - Z_{i,\,j+1}) \qquad [38]$$

where equations 8a and 32 apply and

$$Z_{ij} = 1 \text{ if } i = j$$

$$= 0 \text{ otherwise} \qquad [39]$$

This model is interpreted much the same way as the model that includes diagonal cells. The UA parameter (b_0) is the slope of the line connecting Φ_{1j} to Φ_{Rj}; it measures the effect of an increase in origins on the odds on destination j relative to destination j + 1. However, as in the row effects model, not all expected logits lie along the line between Φ_{ij} and Φ_{Rj}. The diagonal effects parameters shift logits near the diagonal upward or downward (depending on the sign of d_i and whether i = j or i = j + 1).

Quasi-row effects, quasi-column effects, quasi-Model I, quasi-Model II, and quasi-homogeneous row and column effects models can be defined in a similar way:

$$\Phi_{ij} = a_{2j} - a_{2,\,j+1} + b_0 X_i + b_{1i} + d_i(Z_{ij} - Z_{i,\,j+1}) \qquad [40]$$

$$\Phi_{ij} = a_{2j} - a_{2,\,j+1} + (b^0 + b_{2j}) X_i + d_i(Z_{ij} - Z_{i,\,j+1}) \qquad [41]$$

$$\Phi_{ij} = a_{2j} - a_{2,\,j+1} + (b_0 + b_{2j}) X_i + b_{1i} + d_i(Z_{ij} - Z_{i,\,j+1}) \qquad [42]$$

$$\Phi_{ij} = a_{2j} - a_{2,\,j+1} + bu_i(v_j \times v_{j+1}) + d_i(Z_{ij} - Z_{i,\,j+1}) \qquad [43]$$

where equations 8a, 32, and 39 apply. In these models, both row effects (b_{1i}) and diagonal effects (d_i) shift logits off the line from Φ_{i1}, to Φ_{iR}. As in the column effects model and Model I, the column effect parameters (b_{2j}) shift the slopes of those lines. Figure 8 shows the differences among the quasi-UA, quasi-row effects, quasi-column effects, and quasi-Model I models as applied to the U.S. data.

The models enumerated thus far do not exhaust the possibilities for this kind of modeling. Some extensions will be considered in Chapter 6. Other models can be defined by imposing constraints on some of the parameters in one of the general models considered here. For example, the d_i in equation 42 may be constrained to a constant d that applies to

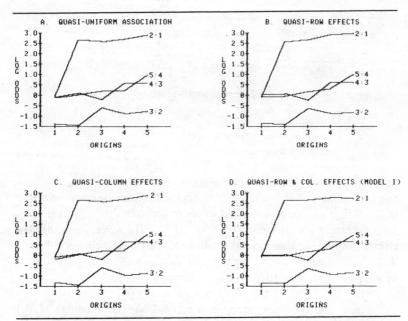

Figure 8: Logits Expected Under Models of Association That Include Diagonal
Parameters

all diagonal cells; another constraint may be placed on a pair of row
effects, e.g., $b_{12} = b_{14}$ in equation 42. Full treatment of constrained
versions of the general models presented here is beyond the scope of
this book, but constraints are important in the applications reviewed
in Chapter 6.

Goodness-of-fit statistics for application of these models to the U.S.
data are in Table 19. Parameter estimates are in Table 19. Fitting the
diagonal cells substantially improves the fit over the comparable
statistics in Table 17. Although all of the models can be rejected at
conventional levels of significance, the fits of the row effects model
and Model I are better than are those of any of the models considered
in preceding sections attained. Column effects appear to be trivial.
Without estimates for Model II, a firm judgment is impossible, but
Model I is not a significant improvement over the row effects model.
Thus the row effects model appears to be the preferred model for the
U.S. data. As panel B of Figure 8 shows, substantial diagonal effects
dwarf the row effects. These diagonal effects peak the odds on a
higher- versus a lower-status destination at immobility for each origin.
However, the positive main effect of origin on destination is also
discernible.

TABLE 18
**Results for Quasi-Association Models of Mobility from
Father's Occupation to Son's First Occupation**

	Destination				
Origin	Upper Nonmanual	Lower Nonmanual	Upper Manual	Lower Manual	Farm
(A) Expected Frequencies: QUA					
Upper Nonmanual	1414	529.70	299.97	641.01	35.33
Lower Nonmanual	638.97	524	297.39	744.57	48.08
Upper Manual	841.64	691.71	856	1577.33	119.33
Lower Manual	861.90	829.93	755.90	3325	230.27
Farm	344.50	388.66	414.75	1670.10	1832
(B) Expected Frequencies: QRCI					
Upper Nonmanual	1414	533.87	278.30	651.80	42.03
Lower Nonmanual	716.37	524	271.66	698.22	42.76
Upper Manual	790.30	661.74	856	1665.56	112.39
Lower Manual	794.30	835.04	812.84	3325	235.82
Farm	386.03	409.35	405.21	1617.41	1832
(C) Expected Frequencies: QHRCI					
Upper Nonmanual	1414	570.64	282.41	612.53	40.41
Lower Nonmanual	678.75	524	276.66	724.94	48.66
Upper Manual	791.25	651.67	856	1669.72	117.36
Lower Manual	825.97	821.84	803.62	3325	226.57
Farm	391.03	395.84	405.31	1625.82	1832

	L^2	X^2	df	p	Δ
QI	683.34	720.74	11	<.01	.055
QUA	73.01	73.45	10	<.01	.020
QRow	34.91	35.08	7	<.01	.011
QColumn	66.69	67.81	7	<.01	.018
QRCI	27.75	27.77	4	<.01	.010
QRCII	24.11	23.78	4	<.01	.013
QHRCI	39.51	39.57	7	<.01	.013
QHRCII	39.28	39.24	7	<.01	.013

Similar Parameters Under Different Models

Take note of the diagonal parameters for the quasi-row effects model in Table 19. The estimated value of d_3 is nearly as large as d_1 and significantly larger than d_2 or d_4. Recall that d_3 was small in the corners and diagonals models, and not significant in the Featherman-Hauser model. The radical difference between estimates is due to the different

TABLE 19

**Parameter Estimates for Quasi-Association Models for Mobility
from Father's Occupation to Son's First Occupation
(Standard Errors in Parentheses)**

Parameter	UA	Row Effects	Column Effects	Row and Column Effects			Homogeneous Effects	
				I	IIa	IIb	I	IIb
Uniform	.158* (.006)	.141* (.008)	.165* (.014)	.109* (.009)	1.621	.158	.118* (.015)	.158
Row								
1	—	0	—	0	.680	5	0	5
2	—	.061* (.030)	—	.040 (.044)	.325	3.863	−.035 (.038)	3.513
3	—	−.053* (.022)	—	−.068* (.028)	−.083	2.560	−.100* (.025)	2.401
4	—	−.100* (.027)	—	.144* (.035)	−.470	1.320	−.136* (.033)	1.313
5	—	0	—	0	−.452	1.379	0	1.193
Column								
1	—	—	0	0	.748	5	0	5
2	—	—	−.036 (.027)	−.044 (.040)	.207	3.269	−.035 (.038)	3.513
3	—	—	−.048 (.033)	−.095* (.038)	−.070	2.383	−.100* (.025)	2.401
4	—	—	−.002 (.041)	−.120* (.050)	−.410	1.297	−.136* (.033)	1.313
5	—	—	0	0	−.475	1.089	0	1.193
Diagonal								
1	.469* (.054)	.503* (.081)	.378* (.072)	.424* (.158)	.086	.086	.308* (.155)	.060
2	.156* (.055)	.108 (.058)	.188* (.061)	.125 (.082)	.275	.275	.135 (.164)	.246
3	.464* (.047)	.490* (.048)	.482* (.048)	.520* (.050)	.527	.527	.812* (.098)	.518
4	.247* (.035)	.100 (.055)	.256* (.036)	.014 (.070)	−.000	−.000	.049 (.067)	.043
5	2.357* (.061)	2.573* (.079)	2.358* (.110)	2.911* (.164)	2.785	2.785	2.910* (.140)	2.763

NOTE: Standard errors could not be calculated for Model II.
*p < .05.

baselines against which d_3 is defined. In the corners, diagonals, and Featherman-Hauser models, the baseline is the model of quasi-perfect mobility; diagonal effects are measured relative to marginal effects that are adjusted for the presence of other interaction effects (Pontinen, 1981). On the other hand, the baseline in the row effects model is the curve that describes the effect of origins on destinations. That curve reflects interaction effects; marginal effects enter only the intercept of the curve. Yet expected frequencies under the different models vary little. Three of the four models reproduce the third diagonal frequency exactly; in the exception—the Featherman-Hauser model—error is less than 10 percent.

. The essential difference between marginal effects and interaction effects as a baseline is clear in the substantive interpretations given the four models. The corners, diagonals, and Featherman-Hauser models state that lower manual occupations are relatively rare destinations for men not from the lower manual or farm strata while upper manual destinations are more common. Furthermore, nonmanual destinations are especially common among men from nonmanual origins. The odds on upper manual destinations are higher for men with upper manual origins than for other men because those other men are pushed toward higher and lower status destinations by special parameters. According to the row effects model, odds on higher-status destinations increase in a curvilinear pattern as origin status increases. When applied to the U.S. data, that pattern suggests little increase in the odds on upper versus lower manual destinations as origin status increases from lower to upper manual. The quasi-row effects model alters the curvilinear pattern by the introduction of the d_i. The estimate of d_3 is large because the odds on an upper manual first job are much higher for men of upper manual origins than the row effects themselves imply.

The preceding paragraph makes two important points. The first point is that to interpret a parameter correctly, the researcher must understand the baseline against which the parameter is calculated. The second point is that the structure of mobility processes cannot be discerned from the expected frequencies under a given model. The substance of any model is in the parameter specification and the estimated values of the parameters. This point brings us back to the discussion of equivalent topological models in the section on Indeterminacy of Topological Models in Chapter 4. The following example—a modification of a point made by Duncan (1978; Duncan and Schuman, 1980, make the point in another context)—elaborates on that earlier discussion.

Equivalent Models—Reprise

Consider two models for a 3 × 3 mobility table. The first model is QPM; the second is a model that includes a UA parameter (b), a homogeneous row-column parameter (c), and a single parameter for all three diagonal cells (d); this model is referred to as the *diagonal row-column model* (DRC) here. Expected frequencies under the two models are given by:

$$\log(F_{ij}) = a_0 + a_{1i} + a_{2j} + d_i Z_{ij} \qquad [44]$$

$$\log(F_{ij}) = a_0 = a_{1i} + a_{2j} + bX_iX_j + c(X_i + X_j) + dZ_{ij} \qquad [45]$$

where equations 8a, 32, and 39 apply.

Both models have three parameters and one degree of freedom. More important, expected frequencies under both models are the same (Duncan, 1978). For that reason the parameters of one model can be expressed as a function of parameters of the other:

QPM as a function of DRC	DRC as a function of QPM
$d_1 = d + 2(b - c)$	$b = (d_1 - 2d_2 + d_3)/6$
$d_2 = d - b$	$c = (d_3 - d_1)/4$
$d_3 = d + 2(b + c)$	$d = (d_1 + 4d_2 + d_3)/6$ [46]

The models are equivalent in a statistical sense only. Substantively they are distinct. QPM posits differences among occupational categories in the density of immobility and independence of origins and destinations for nonstayers. DRC posits uniform density of immobility for all occupational categories and a curvilinear effect of origins on the odds on a higher-status destination. To distinguish between them, the auxiliary rules of symmetry, parsimony, and replicability discussed in Chapter 4 must be invoked. Symmetry and parsimony provide no grounds for a decision as both models are symmetrical and both have three interaction parameters. A decision must be based on replicability.

A Comparison of Mobility in Britain and Denmark

Oft-analyzed 3 × 3 mobility tables from Britain and Denmark are used to apply this concept of replicability. The immediate source of the data is Goodman (1965: 571); the original sources are Glass (1954) and Svalastoga (1959). Categories are simply designated upper, middle, and lower; coding details are available in Goodman (1965). The two tables are treated as a three-way cross-classification (origin by destination by country), and methods described in Clogg (1982a) are used to place cross-national constraints on parameters b, c, and d. Methods described in Goodman (1969b) are used to place cross-national constraints on the QPM parameters.

The analysis focuses on the DRC model; it begins with no cross-national constraints on any of the parameters. Then the b parameters of DRC are constrained to be the same in Britain and Denmark. The c parameters and finally the d parameters are constrained, in turn. These models are designated Model U, Model B, Model C, and Model D (for unconstrained, b constrained, c constrained, and d constrained, respectively). The relationships among the parameters of the DRC shown in equation 46 imply that if Model D is accepted as a preferred model for these data, the d_i must not differ from country to country either. But equation 46 implies nothing about cross-national constraints if Models B or C are preferred. In fact, it is impossible for d_i in Britain to equal d_i in Denmark if Model B or C is true. So if Model B or Model C is preferred, it must be more parsimonious than the corresponding version of QPM, and a clear choice can be made. Similar logic demands that if one or two but not three of the d_i can be constrained across countries, QPM is more parsimonious than DRC.

The results are presented in Table 20. As Goodman noted in his original analysis of these data, QPM fits very well; of necessity, DRC does too. Constraining b, c, and d to be the same in Britain and Denmark does not diminish that fit significantly. The overall increase in L^2 due to the constraints is 2.67 (df = 3; p > .5). The results do not allow a choice between QPM and DRC. Either there is a steep slope (b = .581) that lifts the odds on a higher-status destination for each increase in origins that is modified by a slightly less than expected increase in odds between lower and middle status and modest inheritance in all categories, or there is quasi-perfect mobility with high rates of immobility at the extremes and "disinheritance" in the middle. Much has been made of disinheritance, but I regard it as an unlikely process. Among other things, it does not appear in larger tables. I prefer the DRC model for these data because its parameter values are more plausible.

Duncan's (1979: 801) conclusion is appropriate here:

Model (4) [quasi-uniform association] is especially attractive for comparative research, for the comparison there will take the very sharp form of testing the hypothesis that the model's one parameter for row-by-column interaction is the same in two or more

TABLE 20
Results of Cross-National Comparison of Mobility Models

	U Brit.	U Den.	B Brit.	B Den.	C Brit.	C Den.	D Brit.	D Den.
(A) Goodness of Fit								
L^2	1.44		1.67		2.19		4.11	
X^2	1.44		1.67		2.19		4.10	
df	2		3		4		5	
Δ	.005		.005		.006		.010	
(B) DRC Model Parameters								
b	.563	.599	.578	.578	.578	.578	.581	.581
c	−.099	−.134	−.099	−.135	−.113	−.113	−.115	−.115
d	.175	.218	.164	.235	.164	.240	.191	.191
(C) QPM Parameters Implied by DRC								
d_1	1.501	1.684	1.519	1.660	1.545	1.621	1.583	1.583
d_2	−.388	−.380	−.413	−.343	−.414	−.338	−.390	−.390
d_3	1.103	1.147	1.122	1.122	1.094	1.169	1.122	1.122
(D) Expected log-Odds Ratios								
(θ_{11})	1.113	1.304	1.105	1.317	1.131	1.283	1.193	1.193
(θ_{12})	.388	.380	.413	.343	.414	.338	.390	.390
(θ_{21})	.388	.380	.413	.343	.414	.338	.390	.390
(θ_{22})	.715	.766	.709	.779	.680	.832	.732	.732

populations, or that it varies over time or populations according to some function that the researcher might aspire to specify.

This chapter has demonstrated the power of models of association for summarizing comparative mobility structures.

6. NEW DEVELOPMENTS

The models of the preceding sections can be applied directly to mobility data, but the most interesting recent work has elaborated on these basic models. In this section recent papers by Clogg (1981), Breiger (1981), and Hout (forthcoming) are reviewed. Because each paper presents a unique model, they cannot be discussed en masse. Yet they address several common issues that are worthy of note at the outset, lest the details of the papers conceal the general points. Yamaguchi (1983) and Logan (1983) also address many of these issues; space limitations preclude detailed consideration of their papers.

This first issue is the appropriate level of *aggregation*. Breiger, Yamaguchi, and Hout analyze the 17 × 17 version of the OCG mobility table. Others analyze smaller tables. A subheading under aggregation is the issue of combining occupational categories. Breiger and Goodman (1981) discuss criteria for making combinations.

The second issue is the *treatment of the diagonal*. Most researchers follow the well-established practice of deleting the diagonal or (equivalently) fitting it exactly. Clogg defines latent classes of movers and stayers to account for persistence along the diagonal. Hout models the diagonal explicitly by introducing independent variables to account for the pattern of immobility.

The third issue is the *introduction of independent variables* into the analysis. Yamaguchi, Logan, and Hout share this concern. Yamaguchi and Hout compare mobility patterns among subpopulations; Logan includes formal expressions for the effects of independent variables on mobility structure.

The fourth issue involves the *scaling of occupational categories*. Most researchers use a variant of unit interval scaling such as equation 32. Hout uses means on the Duncan (1961) SEI to score occupational categories.

Fifth, Hout and Yamaguchi raise the possibility of *nonstatus dimensions* of mobility.

Finally, Breiger and Clogg are concerned with class barriers to mobility. Although their approaches are quite distinct, both are engaged in a search for latent social classes. Breiger defines classes in terms of aggregations of occupational categories, whereas Clogg considers class as an oblique dimension that cuts across occupational distinctions; he is more interested in the class composition of the standard categories. Together these six issues form the themes that run through most recent papers on mobility.

Latent Structures of Mobility

Clogg's model is less obviously tied to the models of preceding sections than are the other models under consideration here. Yet as he notes, QPM, the corners model, FH5, and several other fundamental models can be expressed as latent structure models. Both a standard latent structure model (Lazarsfeld and Henry, 1968; Goodman, 1974; Haberman, 1979: 541-552) and a novel quasi-latent structure model are proposed. The basic assertion of latent structure analysis is that one or more unobserved variables account for the association between observed variables. In the context of mobility analysis that means that origins and destinations are independent, conditional on their mutual association with the unobserved variable. Clogg is interested in finding one or more latent variables to explain the relationship between origins and destinations in Britain and Denmark. In this section I add a comparison with the U.S. data to Clogg's analysis.

Let π_{ij} be the expected proportion of cases in cell (i, j) of the mobility table, i.e., $\pi_{ij} = F_{ij}/N$ where F_{ij} is defined by some model (as yet unspecified). Let t index the categories of the unobserved third variable (Z) and π_{ijt}^{XYZ} be the expected proportion in cell (i, j, t) of the unobservable three-way cross-classification. The observable proportions (π_{ij}) are obtained by summing π_{ijt}^{XYZ} over the categories of Z:

$$\pi_{ij} = \sum_t \pi_{ijt}^{XYZ} \qquad [47]$$

The basic latent structure model can be written in terms of the marginal distribution of the latent variable (π_t^Z) and the conditional probabilities that a randomly chosen member of latent class t will have origin i (π_{it}^{XZ}) and destination j (π_{jt}^{YZ}):

$$\pi_{ijt}^{XYZ'} = \pi_t^Z \; \pi_{it}^{XZ} \; \pi_{jt}^{YZ} \qquad [48]$$

Substituting equation 48 into equation 47 yields the "fundamental equation of latent structure analysis" (Clogg, 1981: 839):

$$\pi_{ij} = \sum_t \pi_t^Z \; \pi_{it}^{XZ} \; \pi_{jt}^{YZ} \qquad [49]$$

Note that this model does not posit separate marginal and interaction effects like the other models do. Both observed marginals and observed interactions are considered to be manifestations of latent distributions and interactions. The population is hypothesized to be distributed across the latent classes (in this case there are five latent classes). Given membership in one of the latent classes, an individual has a fixed probability of having one of the four possible origins and one of the five possible destinations. The observed interaction pattern simply reflects the underlying marginals and conditional probabilities. This is a problematic aspect of latent structure models. Although latent classes can be defined so that observed marginals are fit, the model's parameters do not necessarily separate marginal from interaction effects. The observed marginals are attributed to the latent marginals and the interaction between latent and observed variables.

Clogg considers a number of models for the 5×5 British and Danish mobility tables and the 8×8 British mobility table. His preferred models for both 5×5 tables contain five latent classes. The first two classes are latent upper and lower classes defined by constraining $\pi_{it}^{XZ} = 0$ for i = 5 and t = 1, i.e., by excluding men from the lowest origin category from latent class 1, and $\pi_{it}^{XZ} = 0$ for j = 1 and t = 2, i.e., by excluding men from the highest origin category from latent class 2. The other three latent classes consist of latent "stayers" in occupational categories 1, 3, and 5. These latent classes are defined by constraining $\pi_{it}^{XZ} = \pi_{jt}^{YZ} = 1$ for i = j = 1 and t = 3, for i = j = 3 and t = 4, and for i = j = 5 and t = 5.

Results are presented in Table 21. The model attains a borderline fit to the British data and it fits the Danish data very well, but it does not fit the U.S. data as well as some of the other models do. The odds on being a member of the latent upper class are about 20 percent less in Britain (.220/.691 = .318) than in Denmark (.251/.624 = .402) and about

TABLE 21
Five Latent Class Model of Mobility from Father's Occupation to Son's Current Occupation in Britain and Denmark and from Father's Occupation to Son's First Occupation in USA

Index*	Proportion in Latent Class (π_t^z)	Conditional Probability of Origin i Given Latent Class t (π_{i1}^{XZ})	(π_{i2}^{XZ})	Conditional Probability of Destination j Given Latent Class t (π_{j1}^{YZ})	(π_{j2}^{YZ})
(A) Britain					
1	.220	.111	0	.077	.000
2	.691	.509	.043	.438	.063
3	.012	.178	.137	.165	.117
4	.014	.202	.560	.254	.510
5	.062	0	.260	.067	.310
(B) Denmark					
1	.251	.071	0	.084	.010
2	.624	.450	.032	.383	.022
3	.006	.342	.242	.375	.195
4	.059	.137	.466	.125	.505
5	.059	0	.260	.032	.269
(C) USA					
1	.296	.378	0	.342	.129
2	.567	.348	.018	.233	.141
3	.031	.249	.199	.122	.136
4	.019	.015	.524	.285	.556
5	.086	0	.260	.018	.039

*Index represents the values of t in π_t^Z, i in π_{i1}^{XZ} and π_{iz}^{XZ}, and j in π_{j1}^{YZ} and π_{j2}^{YZ}.

40 percent less in Britain than in the United States (.296/.567 = .522). The conditional probability of having an upper nonmanual origin or destination given membership in the upper class is much higher in the United States than in the other two countries. It is not clear whether these differences reflect substantive differences in the stratification processes of the three societies, temporal effects (the European studies predate the U.S. ones by more than twenty years), or coding differences. Regardless of cause, the differences in conditional probabilities reflect differences in observed *marginals*. It is unclear whether or not they reflect differences in the pattern of interactions as well. Conditional distributions of the lower class do not differ much from country to country.

Inferring Class Structure from Mobility Patterns

Breiger (1981) proposes a model that simultaneously combines categories of a large (17 × 17) mobility table into a smaller number of aggregates and estimates the parameters of association among those aggregates. Employing Weber's definition of a social class as the "totality of class situations in which individual and generational mobility is easy and typical" (quoted by Breiger, 1981: 579), Breiger defines a social class as an aggregate of occupational categories selected so that destinations are independent of origins within subtables defined by the intersection of such classes. The procedure is this:

(1) Partition the R occupational categories in the table into C classes. Apply the partition to the rows and columns of the R × R table simultaneously, forming C^2 subtables.
(2) Fit the model of perfect mobility in subtables that contain no diagonal cells; fit the model of quasi-perfect mobility in subtables that contain diagonal cells. Sum the L^2 and degrees of freedom from each subtable to test the null hypothesis that origins are independent of destinations within "classes."
(3) If the null hypothesis of independence within classes cannot be rejected, sum the frequencies in each subtable, forming an aggregated C × C table. Fit the analysis of association models of Chapter 5 to the C × C table.

Breiger tries several partitions suggested by the literature but arrives at a new eight-class partition for the 17 × 17 table for mobility from father's occupation to son's first occupation from OCG-II (a disaggregated version of Table 1). The classes combine the following categories from the seventeen-category classification in Figure 1: (1), (2, 3, 4), (5), (6, 7), (9, 10), (8, 13, 14), (11, 12, 15), and (16, 17).

TABLE 22
L^2 for the 33 Components of Breiger's Model 2 for Mobility
from Father's Occupation to Son's First Occupation

Class	I	II	III	IV	V	VI	VII	VIII
				Breiger's Class Label				
I	–	–	–	–	–	–	–	–
II	–	1.88 (1)*	–	2.02 (2)	1.80 (4)	5.33 (2)	8.94 (4)	1.86 (1)
III	–	–	–	–	–	–	–	–
IV	–	4.78 (2)	–	–	.55 (2)	.05 (1)	.05 (2)	1.40 (1)
V	–	.99 (4)	–	1.98 (2)	.04 (1)	1.09 (2)	.62 (4)	8.68** (2)
VI	–	.47 (2)	–	.90 (1)	.22 (2)	–	8.74** (2)	.70 (1)
VII	–	6.18 (4)	–	2.47 (2)	4.21 (4)	1.79 (2)	.27 (1)	.43 (2)
VIII	–	.94 (2)	–	.32 (1)	.22 (2)	3.13 (1)	1.56 (2)	–

*Degrees of freedom in parentheses.
**$p < .05$.

To test the partition, independence or QPM is fit according to Step 2. There are 64 possible tests when eight classes are proposed, but because several classes contain only one or two of the original categories, Breiger's partitioning results in 31 tests with no degrees of freedom. These untestable tables contain 30.2 percent of the sample cases. L^2 and degrees of freedom for the remaining 33 tests are in Table 22. The sum of these statistics is the $L^2 = 76.9$ on 69 degrees of freedom reported by Breiger (1981: 595). The fit is good ($p > .20$). The 187 $[(R - 1)^2 - 69 = 187]$ implicit parameters account for most of the association in the 17×17 table.

Table 23 summarizes Step 3—the analysis of association in the aggregated table. None of the models considered by Duncan (1979) or Goodman (1979a) fits. Breiger modifies the quasi-row effects model by blocking out three cells for men of farm origins—those for farm origin men with destinations in classes IV, V, or VI. That model fits well. Figure 9 shows the expected odds under the model. The diagonal effects predominate; the effects of origin on destination away from the diagonal are barely visible.

There is evidence that Breiger's model may well be obscuring important off-diagonal effects of father's occupation on son's first

TABLE 23
Results for Brieger's Analysis of Mobility from Father's
Occupation to Son's First Occupation

Origin	Destination							
	I	*II*	*III*	*IV*	*V*	*VI*	*VII*	*VIIII*
(A) Expected Frequencies: M6								
I	25	129.02	1.85	48.94	15.86	23.52	19.26	1.56
II	31.66	1222	13.85	460.04	186.95	347.88	357.32	36.29
III	12.35	311.44	33	199.59	84.04	162.02	172.42	18.14
IV	14.75	378.22	7.16	291	107.33	210.43	227.73	24.37
V	15.39	469.42	10.58	440.29	490	523.11	673.47	85.74
VI	18.87	566.74	12.58	515.38	258.50	1464	752.59	94.34
VII	14.00	479.22	12.12	565.76	323.32	846.04	1283	174.54
VIII	11.98	399.94	9.87	344	328	822	902.22	1832

(B) Parameter Estimates

	UA	Row Effects	Column Effects	Row and Column I		M6
				Row	Column	
UA	.067	.082	.058	.071		.078
II	—	−.139	.063	−.109	.044	−.149
III	—	−.098	.044	−.089	.039	−.107
IV	—	−.034	.026	−.025	.022	−.046
V	—	−.125	−.021	−.116	−.026	−.142
VI	—	−.032	−.032	−.027	−.040	−.049
VII	—	−.064	.028	−.049	.013	−.102

	L^2	X^2	df	p	Δ
UA	167.32	166.83	40	< .01	.030
Row	99.81	97.86	34	< .01	.020
Column	124.43	123.92	34	< .01	.024
R&CI	67.95	66.29	28	< .01	.015
M6	39.29	37.80	31	.19	.009

NOTE: Integers indicate cells fitted exactly.

occupation in the U.S. data. Some of the evidence involves the application of the status, autonomy, and training model described below. Other evidence involves Brieger's criteria for aggregating cells of the table into a "class mobility table" (Step 3). Recall that nearly half of the subtables formed to test the aggregation thesis could not be used for the test because they had no degrees of freedom. Goodman (1981) proposes criteria for combining categories that do not result in subtables with no degrees of freedom. Under Goodman's method, if the

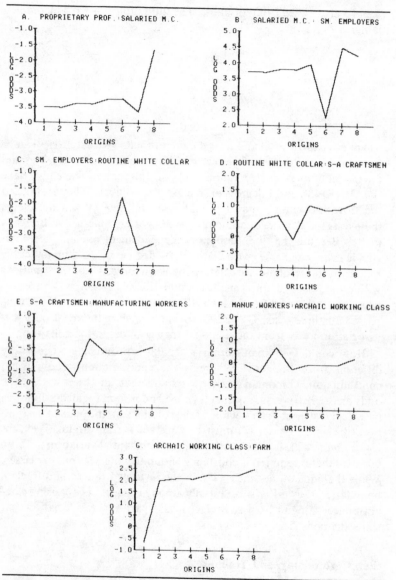

Figure 9: Logits Expected Under Breiger's Model of Class Mobility

researcher wants to test the aggregation thesis for categories 2 and 3, three tables are required. The first table is a 2 × (R − 2) table formed from rows 2 and 3; columns 2 and 3 are deleted from this table. The second table is an (R − 2) × 2 table formed from columns 2 and 3; rows

2 and 3 are deleted from this table. The third table is a 3×3 incomplete table.

$$
\begin{array}{ccc}
- & f_{23} & n_{2.} - f_{22} - f_{23} \\
f_{32} & - & n_{3.} - f_{32} - f_{33} \\
n_{.2} - f_{22} - f_{32} & n_{.3} - f_{23} - f_{33} & -
\end{array}
$$

where n_i is a row total and n_j is a column total. Two categories can be combined if the model of perfect mobility fits the first two tables and the model of quasi-perfect mobility fits the third table. These tests have $(R - 3)$, $(R - 3)$, and 1 degrees of freedom, respectively. They are labeled the "row," "column," and "diagonal" tests in Table 24, which presents these tests for all pairs of occupational categories combined in Breiger's model. Because the three tests are independent of one another, their sum is distributed as χ^2 with $2(R - 3) + 1$ degrees of freedom under the null hypothesis of no association between origins and destinations within the "class" defined by the combination of categories. The results using these criteria differ dramatically from Breiger's results. No pairing passes all three tests. QPM fits all but two. For the most part it is association away from the diagonal that gets lost in the collapsing.

How could Goodman's criteria produce an outcome so radically different from Breiger's? Where is the contradiction? There is no contradiction. Goodman's criteria require that, in the row test, the odds on origin (i) versus another (i') must be constant for all destinations (j) except (j = i) and (j = i'), while in the column test, the odds of destination (j) versus another (j') must be constant for all origins (i) except (i = j) and (i = j'). Breiger's criteria allow substantial variation in those odds; all that is required is constancy within the intersections of classes. While the odds do not differ within the restricted ranges of intraclass boundaries, they differ substantially among classes. In collapsing categories according to Step 2, Breiger masks part of the association that shifts the odds from class to class.

Status, Autonomy, and Training
in Occupational Mobility

Hout's (forthcoming) approach to modeling the mobility table is quite different from Clogg's or Breiger's. The paper is concerned with three things: the arbitrariness of the scoring index in Duncan (1979) and Goodman (1979a), the use of independent variables to account for immobility patterns, and the importance of occupational characteristics other than status for the structure of occupational mobility in large (17 × 17) tables. Haberman's (1974) linear-by-linear interaction model (equation 31) adopts the usual single unit scaling of categories as in equation 32 only as a convenience. Any known scores can be inserted.

TABLE 24
Goodman's Criteria for Combining Categories Applied
to Breiger's Classes

Categories	Row (df = 14)	Column (df = 14)	Diagonal (df = 1)	Total (df = 29)
Class II				
Salaried Professionals with Managers	33.05*	19.77	.08	52.90*
Salaried Professionals with Nonretail Sales	16.98	37.17*	.05	54.20*
Managers with Nonretail Sales	7.63	5.94	4.06*	17.63
Class IV				
Clerks with Retail Sales	13.22	37.80*	.35	51.37*
Class V				
Crafts, other with Crafts, construction	26.86*	34.66*	.25	61.77*
Class VI				
Crafts, manufacturing with Operatives, manufacturing	47.43*	29.24*	1.07	77.74*
Crafts, manufacturing with Labor, manufacturing	78.07	52.39*	1.83	132.29*
Operatives, manufacturing with Labor, manufacturing	27.78*	20.16	.09	48.03*
Class VII				
Service with Operatives, nonmanufacturing	21.05	32.59*	1.76	55.40*
Service with labor, nonmanufacturing	42.96*	43.32*	2.85	89.13*
Operatives, nonmanufacturing with Labor, nonmanufacturing	23.44*	24.56*	.07	48.07*
Class VIII				
Farmers with Farm Labor	34.80*	32.36*	23.19*	90.35*

*p < .05.

The occupational characteristic of greatest concern is occupational status, so equation 32 is supplanted by:

$$X_i = S_i \qquad \text{and} \qquad X_j = S_j$$

where S_i and S_j are the mean SEI (Duncan, 1961) scores for occupational categories i and j. Additional dimensions are added to the model by defining similar terms:

A_i: minus one times the odds on having a supervisor for men in occupation i

T_i: mean specific vocational training for men in occupation i

where both variables are estimated using pooled samples from the General Social Survey, 1972-1980 (NORC, 1980; see Hout, forthcoming, for details).

In addition, diagonal effects are added by employing dummy variables (Z_i) that equal one for diagonal cells and zero otherwise as in equation 40. When the dummy variables are multiplied by a function of the scaled variables (status, autonomy, or training), the coefficient for that effect represents the departure of the diagonal cell from the pattern of interaction elsewhere in the table. This approach differs from the usual "quasi" models that fit the diagonal cells with R variables. In this model there are only three variables for the diagonal. These three variables assert that the deviation of the observed diagonal frequency for a given category from the pattern of interactions away from the diagonal is proportional to the status, autonomy, and training of the occupations in that category.

Expected frequencies under the model are:

$$\log(F_{ij}) = a_0 + a_{1i} + a_{2j} + b_1 S_i S_j + b_2 A_i A_j$$
$$+ d_1 Z_i S_{i2} + d_2 Z_i A_{i2} + d_3 Z_i T_i \qquad [50]$$

where $D_i = 1$ if $i = j$ and 0 otherwise. Notice that the T_i are not included among the main effects, nor do they get squared in the diagonal effects. Preliminary analyses found that the main effect is trivial and that the linear form fits better than T_i^2. Four terms are included in the model but not in the equations. Dummy variables tap the less-than-expected mobility into and out of farming. The four variables allow for differences in mobility patterns for moves between farm and (1) upper nonmanual, (2) lower nonmanual, (3) upper manual, and (4) lower manual. The effects are assumed to be symmetric; i.e., the same effect pertains whether farming is the origin or the destination.

TABLE 25
Results for SAT Model of Mobility from Father's Occupation
to Son's First Occupation by Race and Year

		1962		1973	
		White	*Black*	*White*	*Black*
(A) Main Effects					
Status	(b_1)	.735*	.430*	.618*	.642*
Autonomy	(b_2)	.450*	.783*	.354*	.310*
(B) Diagonal Effects					
Status	(d_1)	−.202*	−.250	−.194*	−.096
Autonomy	(d_2)	.142*	.028	.100*	.155
Training	(d_3)	.221*	.168*	.201*	.154*
(C) Goodness of Fit					
L^2		529.38	228.05	631.51	161.33
X^2		555.24	321.19	660.24	158.96
df		247	247	247	247
p		$<.05$	$>.50$	$<.05$	$>.50$
Δ		.075	.143	.046	.089
N		10,022	836	18,141	1,833

*$p < .05$

In Hout (forthcoming) the SAT model is applied to mobility from
father's occupation to son's current occupation. Table 25 presents the
results for mobility from father's occupation to son's first occupation
for whites and blacks separately (men of other races are excluded) in
both 1962 and 1973. The model does not fit the data for whites, although
the ratio of L^2 to degrees of freedom is comparable to many of the
other models. It does fit the data for blacks. Care must be taken in
interpreting the difference in fit between blacks and whites. Note that
the Δs for blacks and whites are comparable. Small differences in Δs
suggest that the differences in L^2 are more likely due to the differences
in sample size than to substantive differences in the fit of the model.
When the cohorts that make up the total sample are analyzed separately,
the fit for whites in each cohort is acceptable.

The parameter estimates show the expected pattern in all but one
respect. The effects of status and autonomy on overall mobility are
strong and highly significant for both blacks and whites. The effect
of autonomy on immobility is positive for both blacks and whites but
significant for whites only. The effect of training is strong and positive
for both groups in both years. The unexpected result is the negative

effect of status on immobility. The only reason this term is in the equation is as a control for the status component of training.

This model reveals a much more substantial effect of status on intergenerational mobility than Breiger's model detects. Furthermore, it accounts for most of the diagonal association as an outcome of differential training and autonomy of the occupations while Breiger's model simply deletes the diagonal. Finally, this model is far more parsimonious: It fits 9 interaction parameters while Breiger's model fits 195.

7. APPLICATIONS OF MOBILITY TABLES TO FAMILY AND RELIGION

The identity between row and column categories that distinguishes mobility tables can be found in other subject areas, too. When rows and columns are the same, many of the models described in this book can be applied. When the categories are also ordered, all of the models are applicable. In this final section, I take the opportunity to review four applications of mobility table methodology to other matters.

Occupations of Husbands and Wives

The cross-classification of husbands' and wives' occupations in two-earner families looks very much like a mobility table. Not only are rows and columns identical; they are identical occupational classifications. But in a mobility table the rows and columns refer to one person's statuses at two points in time. In a husband-wife table, one person's status is cross-classified with another's at one point in time. Hout (1982) analyzes the association between husbands' and wives' occupations in March 1978. Table 26 summarizes that analysis.

In the mobility table the temporal ordering of origins and destinations makes it clear which variable is cause and which is effect. In the husband-wife table, no such causal ordering exists. The influence is mutual, or the association may be due to common exogenous causes like assortative marriage by education and social class. This causal symmetry makes modeling symmetry a priority. Special attention is given to the symmetrical models of association: uniform association and the homogeneous versions of Model I and Model II. As the last panel of Table 26 shows, homogeneous Quasi-Model I is the preferred model for these data.

Most of the association between husbands' and wives' occupations is on the diagonal; the difference in L^2 between perfect mobility and

TABLE 26
Analysis of Association Between Husbands' and Wives' Occupations
in Two-Earner Families: March 1978

Husband's Occupation	Wife's Occupation				
	Upper Nonmanual	Lower Nonmanual	Blue Collar	Service	Farm
(A) Observed Frequencies					
Upper Nonmanual	1,708	1,872	236	416	26
Lower Nonmanual	405	836	142	192	3
Blue Collar	741	2,242	1,297	1,125	34
Service	149	279	112	245	3
Farm	62	97	34	67	114
(B) Expected Frequencies: Homogeneous Model I					
Upper Nonmanual	1,708	1,877.55	230.34	422.03	20.08
Lower Nonmanual	398.61	836	145.31	192.86	5.22
Blue Collar	751.68	2,233.67	1,297	1,121.68	34.97
Service	135.44	291.53	110.30	245	5.73
Farm	71.27	87.25	38.05	63.43	114
(C) Parameter Estimates: Homogeneous Model I					
UA	−.090*				
Row & Column		.299*	−.108*	−.175*	

Model	L^2	X^2	df	p
PM	2263.38*	3921.35*	16	< .05
QPM	364.14*	368.14*	11	< .05
QUA	151.78*	163.07*	10	< .05
Q-Row	78.70*	85.68*	7	< .05
Q-Column	111.45*	110.96*	7	< .05
Q-Model I	5.30	5.08	4	.18
Q-Model II	14.73*	10.49*	4	< .05
Q-Homogeneous (I)	9.78	9.49	7	.20
Q-Homogeneous (II)	19.38*	15.56*	7	< .05

*p < .05.

QPM is 1,899.24 with 5 degrees of freedom. The rest of the association is captured by the homogeneous row-column effects and a slightly negative UA parameter. The column effect rotates that negative UA to a positive slope for the odds on lower nonmanual relative to blue collar, but the slope is negative for the odds on service relative to farm and upper nonmanual relative to lower nonmanual. Note, however, that the slopes are net of substantial diagonal effects, particularly for upper nonmanual and farm, so the negative slopes for the off-diagonal

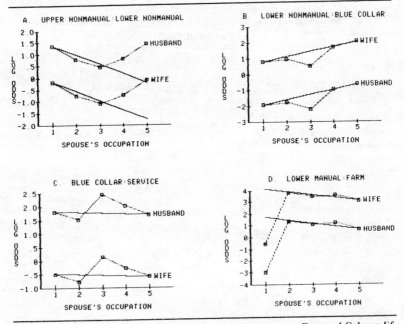

Figure 10: Logits Expected Under the Model of Homogeneous Row and Column Effects (Model I) for the Association of Husbands' and Wives' Occupations

association simply correct for huge diagonal effects at the extremes of the status hierarchy. The relationships are clear in Figure 10. The broken lines show the hypothetical relationship based on UA and column effects only; the solid lines connect the expected frequencies under the complete model. The differences between broken and solid lines demonstrate the importance of row and diagonal effects.

Religious Assortative Marriage

Some may view the husband-wife association in Table 26 as an expression of assortative marriage. But the occupations in that table are current occupations, so they reflect not only assortative marriage but also events since marriage. Nonetheless, mobility models are ideal for the study of assortative marriage if premarriage data for spouses are available. Johnson (1980) presents an excellent example of that kind of application of mobility models to data on religious assortative marriage. Taking data on spouses' religions at age 16, he modifies the crossings parameters model of Chapter 3 to achieve new insight into the importance of religion for the marriage market.

Recall that the crossings parameters model proposes a boundary between adjacent categories. The permeability of that boundary is represented by a parameter (v_s). The frequency expected in cell (i, j) is a function of the number of boundaries that must be crossed in traversing the distance between i and j. To apply the model, the categories must be uniquely ordered so that it is clear which boundaries are traversed for each pair of rows and columns.

Religious categories are not normally ordered. However, Johnson (1980: 69-89) proposes an order based on the ranking of "cognitive social distances" among religious groups described by Rokeach (1960). Rokeach found that Baptists and Catholics are the most cognitively distant religious groups in the community of Lansing, Michigan. Furthermore, he found that the four other groups he studied (Methodists, Presbyterians, Lutherans, and Episcopalians) could be arrayed on a undimensional scale along a line connecting Baptists and Catholics. With one modification (combining Episcopalians and Presbyterians), Johnson applies this order and fits crossings parameters to intermarriage among these groups. But these groups do not exhaust the religious affiliations of the general American population. The remaining religious preferences (including "none") are grouped together in a large residual category, which Johnson treats as equidistant to the "mainline" Christian groups.

The two models proposed by Johnson are charted in Table 27. Note that he constrains the marginal effects to be the same for rows and columns and that the interaction effects are symmetrical. The models differ only in the treatment of the diagonal. The first (CFS) constrains the diagonal effect ("intrinsic endogamy") to be the same for each group; the second (CS) relaxes this constraint. Both models include crossings parameters for each boundary between mainline groups and a single crossings parameter for the "other" row and column. Johnson analyzes four data sets. I will review his results for only one: the NORC general social surveys of 1973-1976 (NORC, 1980). The CFS model fits at the .05 level but CS significantly improves that fit. The estimates of the parameters are in Table 28. Also included are two derived parameters calculated by Johnson: the proportion of the population in each group (p_i) and the implied proportion of each group marrying a member of the group (I_i). The greatest intrinsic endogamy is in the "other" group. The endogamy of the Lutherans is also high. The greatest distance separates the Methodists and the combined Presbyterian-Episcopalian group. The main difference between the CS and CFS models is in the estimates of intrinsic endogamy of the "other" group and of the social distance between the "other" group and the mainline groups. CFS constrains intrinsic endogamy to be the same in all groups.

TABLE 27
Parameterization of Interaction Effects in CFS and CS Models of Religious Assortative Marriage

Respondent's Religion at Age 16	Spouse's Religion at Age 16					
	Baptist	Methodist	Presbyterian	Lutheran	Catholic	Other
(A) CFS Model						
Baptist	m^*	V_{bm}	$V_{bm} + V_{mp}$	$V_{bm} + V_{mp} + V_{pl}$	$V_{bm} + V_{mp} + V_{pl} + V_{lc}$	V_o
Methodist	V_{bm}	m^*	V_{mp}	$V_{mp} + V_{pl}$	$V_{mp} + V_{pl} + V_{lc}$	V_o
Presbyterian	$V_{bm} + V_{mp}$	V_{mp}	m^*	V_{pl}	$V_{pl} + V_{lc}$	V_o
Lutheran	$V_{bm} + V_{mp} + V_{pl}$	$V_{mp} + V_{pl}$	V_{pl}	m^*	V_{lc}	V_o
Catholic	$V_{bm} + V_{mp} + V_{pl} + V_{lc}$	$V_{mp} + V_{pl} + V_{lc}$	$V_{pl} + V_{lc}$	V_{lc}	m^*	V_o
Other	V_o	V_o	V_o	V_o	V_o	m^*
(B) CS Model						
Baptist	m_b	V_{bm}	$V_{bm} + V_{mp}$	$V_{bm} + V_{mp} + V_{pl}$	$V_{bm} + V_{mp} + V_{pl} + V_{lc}$	V_o
Methodist	V_{bm}	m_m	V_{mp}	$V_{mp} + V_{pl}$	$V_{mp} + V_{pl} + V_{lc}$	V_o
Presbyterian	$V_{bm} + V_{mp}$	V_{mp}	m_p	V_{pl}	$V_{pl} + V_{lc}$	V_o
Lutheran	$V_{bm} + V_{mp} + V_{pl}$	$V_{mp} + V_{pl}$	V_{pl}	m_l	V_{lc}	V_o
Catholic	$V_{bm} + V_{mp} + V_{pl} + V_{lc}$	$V_{mp} + V_{pl} + V_{lc}$	$V_{pl} + V_{lc}$	V_{lc}	m_c	V_o
Other	V_o	V_o	V_o	V_o	V_o	m_o

NOTE: Both models contain symmetric marginal effects.

TABLE 28

Parameter Estimates and Derived Quantities for CFS and CS Models
of Religious Assortative Marriage: United States, 1973-1976

Parameter	Baptist	Methodist	Presbyterian	Lutheran	Catholic	Other
			Religious Category			
(A) CFS Model						
Marginal Effects	.636	.154	−.249	.047	.668	−
Diagonal Effects	.786	.786	.786	.786	.786	.786
Crossings Effects		−.255	−.413	−.389	−.171	−.918
Proportion of Pop.	.26	.15	.09	.12	.28	.10
Proportion In-marrying	.61	.42	.31	.36	.62	.45
(B) CS Model						
Marginal Effects	.303	−.135	−.633	−.565	.203	−
Diagonal Effects	.661	.450	.750	1.198	.936	1.944
Crossings Effects		−.339	−.449	−.363	−.075	−.340
Proportion of Pop.	.26	.15	.09	.12	.28	.10
Proportion In-marrying	.61	.37	.30	.42	.62	.45

NOTE: Marginal effects apply to both rows and columns due to imposed symmetry.

This model ascribes a high social distance from "other" to mainline. Relaxing the constraint on intrinsic endogamy allows it to increase for "others," and the model compensates by reducing the estimates of social distance from "other" to the mainline.

Religious Socialization

The association between religious origins and destinations is explored by McRae (1979). McRae's analysis is interesing for two reasons. First is the obvious substantive interest. Second is the formal issue of introducing additional variables into the analysis. McRae estimates the effects of both fathers' and mothers' religious preferences on the religious preferences of adult men and women in Detroit in 1958 and 1971. He considers three categories of religion: Protestant, Catholic, and others. In its most general form, McRae's model is a sex-specific model of pairwise diagonal effects, i.e., it contains a mother's effect that operates on those cells in which mother's and respondents have the same religion, an analogous father's effect, and a homogamy effect that operates on cells in which all three religions are the same. The model is charted in Table 29. Expected frequencies and parameter estimates are in Table 30. Note that McRae constrained many of the parameters.

TABLE 29
Parameterization of McRae's Pairwise Diagonal Model of Intergenerational Religious Transmission (multiplicative form)

Father's Religion	Mother's Religion	Respondent's Religion		
		Protestant	Catholic	Other
Protestant	Protestant	$d_{pt}m_{pt}h_{pt}q$	1	1
	Catholic	d_{pt}	$m_{ct}q$	1
	Other	d_{pt}	1	m_{ot}
Catholic	Protestant	m_{pt}	d_{ct}	1
	Catholic	1	$d_{ct}m_{ct}h_{ct}$	1
	Other	1	d_{ct}	m_{ot}
Other	Protestant	m_{pt}	1	d_{ot}
	Catholic	1	m_{ct}	d_{ot}
	Other	1	1	$d_{ot}m_{ot}h_{ot}$

NOTE: The model fits the father's religion by mother's religion by year marginals and the respondent's religion by year marginals. d refers to the effect of father's religion for a given religion and year, m refers to the effect of mother's religion for a given religion and year, and h refers to a homogamy effect for given religion and year.

TABLE 30
Parameter Estimates for McRae's Model of Intergenerational Religious Transmission

Parameter	Year	Respondent's Religion		
		Protestant	Catholic	Other
Father (d)	1958	17	5.9	2.2
	1971	1.7	5.9	2.2
Mother (m)	1958	4.3	5.9	2.2
	1971	4.3	5.9	2.2
Homogamy (h)	1958	1.0	1.0	7.5
	1971	1.0	1.0	1.0

NOTE: Coefficients are in multiplicative form (1.0 means no significant effect). Identical entries are constrained to be equal.

The principal finding is the existence of a significant effect of both parents' religious preferences on the preferences of their offspring. Mothers' and fathers' effects are important and unchanging for both men and women. Mother's effects are greater than father's effects. Parental homogamy intensifies the socializing influence of parents on children of "other" religions in 1958.

8. CONCLUSION

So concludes this survey of models for mobility tables and similar cross-classifications. The primary ground for extending the work summarized there is in the integration of tabular and regression methods. Duncan, Breiger, Hout, and Logan are all moving in that direction. More work remains. Significant work is also anticipated in the application of these models to new substantive areas. Parental influences on political preferences are strong (Knoke, 1976). Husbands and wives share many attributes that can be studied using these methods. Panel studies also lend themselves to this modeling strategy.

Finally, multivariate modeling is an emerging issue. Yamaguchi, Hout, and Logan all consider exogenous influences on the mobility process. More work on the incorporation of constrained effects of exogenous variables needs to be done. This is a particularly important area for mobility research. It is my hope that this book simulates work on those topics.

REFERENCES

BARON, J. N. (1980) "Indianapolis and beyond: a structural model of occupational mobility across generations." American Journal of Sociology 85: 815-839.

BISHOP, Y.M.M., S. E. FIENBERG, and P. W. HOLLAND (1975) Discrete Multivariate Analysis: Theory and Practice. Cambridge, MA: MIT Press.

BLAU, P. M. and O. D. DUNCAN (1967) The American Occupational Structure. New York: John Wiley.

BLUMEN, I., M. KOGAN, and P. T. McCARTHY (1955) The Industrial Mobility of Labor as a Probability Process. Ithaca, NY: Cornell University Press.

BOUDON, R. (1975) Mathematical Structures of Social Mobility. New York: Elsevier.

BREIGER, R. L. (1981) "The social class structure of occupational mobility." American Journal of Sociology 87: 578-611.

CLOGG, C. C. (1983) Introduction to Structural Models for Qualitative Data. New York: Academic.

——— (1982a) "The analysis of association models for social data." Journal of the American Statistical Association 77: 803-815.

——— (1982b) "Using association models in sociological tables." American Journal of Sociology 88: 114-134.

——— (1981) "Latent structure models for mobility tables." American Journal of Sociology 86: 836-852.

DAVIS, J. A. (1974) "Hierarchical models for significance tests in multivariate contingency tables," pp. 189-231 in H. L. Costner (ed.) Sociological Methodology, 1973-74. San Francisco: Jossey-Bass.

DUNCAN, O. D. (1981) "Two faces of panel analysis: parallels with comparative cross-sectional analysis and time-lagged association," pp. 281-318 in S. Leinhardt (ed.) Sociological Methodology, 1981. San Francisco: Jossey-Bass.

——— (1979) "How destination depends on origin in the occupational mobility table." American Journal of Sociology 84: 793-803.

——— (1978) Personal communication.

——— (1966) "Methodological issues in the analysis of social mobility," pp. 51-97 in N. J. Smelser and S. M. Lipset (eds.) Social Structure and Economic Development. Chicago: Aldine.

——— (1961) "A socioeconomic index for all occupations," pp. 109-138 in A. J. Reiss, Jr. (ed.) Occupations and Social Structure. Glencoe, IL: Free Press.

——— and H. SCHUMAN (1980) "Effects of question wording and context: an experiment with religious indicators." Journal of the American Statistical Association 75: 269-275.

FEATHERMAN, D. L. and R. M. HAUSER (1978) Opportunity and Change. New York: Academic.

————— M. SOBEL, and P. DICKENS (1975) "A manual for coding occupations." Center for Demography and Ecology, Paper 75-1, University of Wisconsin.

FIENBERG, S. E. (1980) The Analysis of Cross-Classified Categorical Data. Cambridge, MA: MIT Press.

GLASS, D. V. (1954) Social Mobility in Britain. London: Routledge & Kegan Paul.

GOLDBERGER, A. S. (1973) "Structural equation models," pp. 1-18 in A. S. Goldberger and O. D. Duncan (eds.) Structural Equation Models in the Social Sciences. New York: Seminar.

GOLDTHORPE, J. W. and K. HOPE (1971) "Occupational grading and occupational prestige," pp. 17-79 in K. Hope (ed.) The Analysis of Social Mobility: Methods and Approaches. Oxford: Clarendon.

GOODMAN, L. A. (1981) "Criteria for determining whether certain categories in a cross-classification table should be combined." American Journal of Sociology 87: 612-650.

————— (1979a) "Simple models for the analysis of association in cross-classifications having ordered categories." Journal of the American Statistical Association 74: 537-352.

————— (1979b) "Multiplicative models of the analysis of mobility tables and other kinds of cross-classification tables." American Journal of Sociology 84: 804-819.

————— (1974) "The analysis of systems of qualitative variables when some of the variables are unobservable." American Journal of Sociology 79: 1179-1259.

————— (1972a) "Some multiplicative models for the analysis of cross-classified data," pp. 649-696 in J. Neymann (ed.) Proceedings of the Sixth Berkeley Symposium on Mathematical Statistics and Probability. Berkeley: University of California Press.

————— (1972b) "A modified regression approach to the analysis of dichotomous variables." American Sociological Review 37: 28-46.

————— (1972c) "A general model for the analysis of surveys." American Journal of Sociology 77: 1035-1086.

————— (1969a) "How to ransack social mobility tables and other kinds of cross-classification tables." American Journal of Sociology 75: 1-39.

————— (1969b) "On the measurement of social mobility: An index of status persistence." American Sociological Review 34: 831-850.

————— (1968) "The analysis of cross-classified data: independence, quasi-independence, and interaction in contingency tables with or without missing entries." Journal of the American Statistical Association 63: 1091-1131.

————— (1965) "On the statistical analysis of mobility tables." American Journal of Sociology 70: 564-585.

————— (1961) "Statistical methods for the mover-stayer model." Journal of the American Statistical Association 56: 841-868.

HABERMAN, S. J. (1979) Analysis of Qualitative Data. 2 vols. New York: Academic.

————— (1974) "Log-linear models for frequency tables with ordered classifications." Biometrics 30: 589-600.

HAUSER, R. M. (1981) "Hope for the mobility ratio." Social Forces 60: 572-584.

————— (1979) "Some exploratory methods for modeling mobility tables and other cross-classified data, pp. 141-458 in D. R. Heise (ed.) Sociological Methodology, 1980. San Francisco: Jossey-Bass.

————— (1978) "A structural model of the mobility table." Social Forces 56: 919-953.

———— P. J. DICKINSON, H. P. TRAVIS, and J. M. KOFFEL (1975a) "Structural changes in occupational mobility among men in the United States." American Sociological Review 40: 585-598.

———— (1975b) "Temporal changes in occupational mobility: evidence for men in the United States." American Sociological Review 40: 279-297.

HODGE, R. W. (1981) "The measurement of occupational status." Social Science Research 10: 396-415.

HOUT, M. (forthcoming) "Status, autonomy, and training in occupational mobility."

———— (1982) "The association between husbands' and wives' occupations in two-earner families." American Journal of Sociology 88: 397-409.

JOHNSON, R. A. (1980) Religious Assortative Marriage in the United States. New York: Academic.

KNOKE, D. (1976) Change and Continuity in American Politics. Baltimore: Johns Hopkins University Press.

———— and P. J. BURKE (1980) Log-Linear Models. Sage University Paper series on Quantitative Applications in the Social Sciences, 07-020. Beverly Hills, CA: Sage.

LAZARSFELD, P. F. and N. W. HENRY (1968) Latent Structure Analysis. Boston: Houghton-Mifflin.

LENSKI, G. (1966) Power and Privilege. New York: McGraw-Hill.

LIPSET, S. M. and R. BENDIX (1959) Mobility in Industrial Society. Berkeley: University of California Press.

———— (1952) "Social mobility and career patterns." American Journal of Sociology 57: 494-504.

LOGAN, J. A. (1983) "A multivariate model for the mobility table." American Journal of Sociology 87.

MACDONALD, K. I. (1981) "On the formulation of a structual model of the mobility table." Social Forces 60: 557-571.

McRAE, J. A. (1979) "The stability of religious differences in primary group attitudes and behaviors." Ph.D. dissertation, University of Arizona.

National Opinion Research Center [NORC] (1980) General Social Surveys: Cumulative Codebook. Chicago: National Opinion Research Center and Roper Center.

PONTINEN, S. (1981) "Models and social mobility research: a comparison of some log-linear models for a social mobility matrix." Department of Sociology, University of Helsinki. (mimeo)

PULLUM, T. (1975) Measuring Occupational Inheritance. New York: Elsevier.

ROGOFF, N. (1953) Recent Trends in Occupational Mobility. Glencoe, IL: Free Press.

ROKEACH, M. (1960) The Open and Closed Mind. New York: Basic Books.

SIMON, G. (1974) "Alternative analyses for the singly-ordered contingency table." Journal of the American Statistical Association 69: 971-976.

SINGER, B. and S. SPILERMAN (1976) "The representation of social processes by Markov models." American Journal of Sociology 82: 1-54.

———— (1974) "Social mobility processes for heterogeneous populations," pp. 256-401 in H. L. Costner (ed.) Sociological Methodology, 1973-74. San Francisco: Jossey-Bass.

SVALASTOGA, K. (1959) Prestige, Class, and Society. Copenhagen: Gyldendal.

TYREE, A. (1973) "Mobility ratios and association in mobility tables." Population Studies 27: 577-588.

U.S. Department of Labor (1977) Dictionary of Occupational Titles: Fourth Edition. Washington: Government Printing Office.

WHITE, H. C. (1963) "Cause and effect in social mobility tables." Behavioral Science 7: 14-27.

WRIGHT, E. O. and L. PERRONE (1977) "Marxist class categories and income inequality." American Sociological Review 42: 32-55.

YAMAGUCHI, K. (1983) "The structure of intergenerational occupational mobility: generality and specificity in resources, channels, and barriers." American Journal of Sociology 88: 718-745.

MICHAEL HOUT is Associate Professor of Sociology at the University of Arizona. He has published articles on stratification and demography. His current work is on status, autonomy, and training in occupational mobility and on the demography of two-earner families in the United States.

Quantitative Applications
in the Social Sciences

(a Sage University Papers Series)

$6.50 each

SAGE PUBLICATIONS, INC.
P.O. BOX 5084
NEWBURY PARK, CALIFORNIA 91359—9924

Place
Stamp
here